VIMTO

The Story of a Soft Drink

SUE NICHOLS

Carnegie Publishing, 1994

Sue Nichols (née Johnson) was born in South Australia of British parents in 1954. After studying History and Fine Arts at Sydney University, she moved to London in 1974 to obtain a BA (Hons) and an MA in the History of European Art at the Courtauld Institute of Art, University of London. She then worked as a photo librarian and picture researcher in the record industry and publishing. Her writings include a chapter to update a new edition of *The Larousse Encyclopedia of Modern Art* (1980) and contributions to *A Concise Encyclopaedia of the Italian Renaissance* (1981).

In 1981 Sue met Simon Nichols. The couple married and moved to south Manchester, where Simon had taken up his financial post in the Nichols company. They have two children, Rachel and Paul, who were born in 1987 and 1989 respectively.

In 1990 Sue was responsible for forming the VIMTO Advertising Collection and organising the travelling exhibition upon which this book is based. In 1991 she instigated and coordinated the 'Monument to VIMTO' sculpture project. Her next project is to write an essay on soft drinks in the *Cambridge World History of Food and Nutrition*.

Vimto: The Story of a Soft Drink
Sue Nichols

Published by Carnegie Publishing, 1994

Copyright © Carnegie Publishing Ltd, 1994
Text copyright © Sue Nichols, 1994
Photographs copyright © see Picture Sources

Typeset in Monotype Bembo by Carnegie Publishing Ltd, 18 Maynard St, Preston, Lancashire.
Printed and bound in the UK by The Alden Press, Oxford.

British Library Cataloguing in Publication Data
A CIP record for this book is available from the British Library

ISBN 1-85936-005-X

Contents

Foreword

WRITE a few sparkling words about VIMTO they said. I can't, I said, but I'll tell you how I discovered it. It was New Year's Eve 1952/3 and, as was the custom (though I didn't know it then, being just turned four), I was at my nan's near the boxworks in Warrington. My dad had carried me the three miles on his shoulders. Me and the rest of the kids spent most of the night playing in the bedrooms undisturbed by the adults, who were getting noisier and noisier, until they came and got us and made us all join in a game of Ring a' Ring a' Roses. The adults didn't know the words, so they sang some song about an old man called Lang who lost an eye; then we all had to kiss everybody else, even our sisters. Then drinks were given to everybody; mine was in a little bottle that they got from a wooden box in the snow outside; it had a lid on it that you couldn't get off without a metal thing. When I took a swig it was so cold that I thought it had cut my throat inside, but then the taste came through and I was hooked. It was like drinking apples and oranges, lemons and limes, and those other fruits, like strawberries, raspberries and blackcurrants that your grannie gave you for tea on Sundays in the summer, and yet it was like none of them and all of them at the same time, it was sweet and fizzy like lemonade from the shop, but it was something else. It was magic. I've drunk in most New Years with VIMTO ever since, even when I lived beyond its range in exotic places like Winchester, Newcastle-upon-Tyne, Sydney, Famagusta and Catterick. The magic then was sobering; sometimes it needed to be because it was not always alone in the glass, it conjured up pictures of home, dad, mum, our house, my brother, Spot, the golden gates of Warrington town hall, the rugby match on a Saturday, St Alban's Youth Club, and yes, even my sister. It reminded me of the times that we used to spend five minutes staring at the defused bomb displayed outside the fire station as we made our way from the baths. And how we would call into the Rainbow Café where VIMTO was sold hot or cold and was advertised on the counter by a lamp with a moving train on the shade—how did it work?

Nothing stays the same of course; there have been changes. I was cross when they started putting it in cans. It tasted the same but it didn't seem right. Now they are advertising it on the telly like any ordinary drink. It's an outrage. VIMTO isn't just another drink like the cola that makes Michael Jackson dance; or orange that makes a red fat chap run out and slap you about the face; nor is it made from girders. VIMTO is my childhood in a glass. And another thing; the advertisement says that VIMTO is a sparkling fruit drink. It isn't. VIMTO does not sparkle. It fizzed in 1952, it fizzes now and as far as I'm concerned it will always fizz.

Allan Beswick

Acknowledgements

I would firstly like to thank Carnegie Publishing Ltd for their assistance and patience in the publication of my book.

There are certain people who are indirectly responsible for the project through their support of the VIMTO Advertising Collection including Lucio Santoro of Santoro Graphics, the paper conservator Susie Bioletti, Robert Opie and Jan Garling of the fascinating Museum of Packaging and Advertising in Gloucester, Roy Morgan formerly of *Collectors Mart*, Jocelyn Hill and Adam Dabre of Quarry Bank Mill, Styal who first hosted the travelling exhibition and the Curators at Salford Museum and Art Gallery, Portland Basin Industrial Heritage Centre, Cannock Valley Heritage Centre, Warrington Museum and Art Gallery, Lancaster City Museum, the Bath Industrial Heritage Museum and the Gunnersbury Park Museum, London who have ensured that thousands of people have had a chance to see the VIMTO Advertising Collection first hand before it goes back into storage again.

Many have helped with the contents of the book. In some instances I have quoted them directly or else have incorporated their information and memories into the text. In this context, I would like to thank particularly the sons and daughter of Noel Nichols, Peter, John and Lois Dix, his nephew Noel Nichols and his grandson, John Nichols, the present Managing Director of J. N. Nichols (Vimto) plc. Current members of staff including John Broome, John Burns, Gordon Edwards, Ken Richards, Chris Sefton, Paul Tolley and David Warren have all given me an insight into the workings of the modern company. The associates of the firm, Tom Reddy Advertising, Maley Design & Advertising and JGPR have also provided me with information and visual material. In addition, Joan Bowker has helped me with her recollections and insight into advertising from the recent past.

Former members of staff, Mrs J. A. Bluer, Eileen Brocklehurst, Doreen Dean, Frances Denmeed, Eileen Hudson, Marian Hughes, Alan Isherwood, Brian Kilby, Bill Lee, Dorothy Mayo, Joe Pearson and Marjorie Stevenson have built up the picture of the company over the years. Relatives of the staff including Mr R. D. Boothman, Ruth Kilby and Gordon and Kenneth W. Lees and Thomas Parker have further enlivened the text.

I have had correspondence with or spoken to many members of the public over the past three years about their recollections and stories of VIMTO and the Nichols family. I would like to thank Geoffrey Balding, Brian Blakeway, Miles E. Birtwell, Dorothy Bradbury, B. W. Buttler, Mrs Ann Edgar, Patricia Hayes, Sgt. Terry D. Johnson, Mr J. P. Lissimore, Rod Lister, Eileen Mullis, Julie Plant, Robert M. Scholey, R. G. Simpson, J. A. Taft of Dayla Soft Drinks (Midlands) Ltd, Mrs Alice Turner, Mr and Mrs Waddinton of Herbal

Health, Ms J. L. Wallwork and the Wilson Family of Bank House for their contributions. In particular, I would like to thank Albert Heaviside, who after a chance meeting in a pantomime audience wrote down many fascinating childhood memories for me to dip into. The authors Tom Bridge and Kay Davenport, who gave me much encouragement as well as Helen Currie, Dr David Fowler, Cliff Hayes, Anthony Rea, Geoffrey Shryhane, Barbara Singh and Judy Spours who also deserve thanks. The publisher of many local history books, Neil Richardson, has also been helpful. They all have in their way created the rich past described here.

In conjunction with the 'Monument to VIMTO' project, I would like to thank all the artists involved, especially Kerry Morrison for her energy and artistry. The members of the selection panel, Iain McMullan, Tony Pass, Christopher Rose-Innes and Virginia Tandy also made the project possible. The director of the City Art Gallery, Richard Gray and his staff brought the sculpture competition into the public gaze.

Thanks must also be given to the radio presenter Allan Beswick for his continuing enthusiasm for VIMTO and for the writing of the Foreword. I would also like to give a particular 'thank you' to Jane Kearns, personal assistant to John and Simon Nichols, for skilfully typing the many manuscript drafts amended by my editors and censors. Michael Minifie of Camera Five Four has had the involved and skilled work of preparing the illustrations for reproduction in the book and the exhibition.

Lastly, I would like to save my warmest thanks for my parents Jeanne and Alan Johnson and to my husband Simon for all their love, patience and support. As for my two children, Rachel and Paul, I look forward to the day when they can read and enjoy my book and appreciate why I could not play with them for a little of their childhood.

Picture sources

The majority of illustrations in this book are taken from the VIMTO Advertising Collection and remain the copyright of J. N. Nichols (Vimto) plc, Ledson Road, Manchester, M23 9NL from whom permission must be sought to reproduce them. The following organisations and individuals have kindly allowed the additional illustrations to be reproduced: Mike Arron p. 103b; BFI Stills, Posters and Designs p. 10; Mrs J. A. Bluer p. 12; Documentary Photography Archive pp. 22t, 102t, 110b; The Hulton-Deutsch Collection Ltd. p. 108b; The Directors and University Librarian, The John Rylands University Library of Manchester pp. 11, 115b; University of Central Lancashire, Preston p. 22b; *Manchester Evening News* p. 76t; Mrs E. Mullis p. 94b; National Museum of Photography, Film and Television (the *Daily Herald* Archive) by courtesy of the Board of Trustees of the Science Museum pp. 24t, 106t; The North West Film Archive at The Manchester Metropolitan University p. 113t; The Board of Trustees of the National Museums & Galleries on Merseyside (Stewart Bale Collection) p. 112t; Anthony Rea Collection p.111b; Martin Breese, Retrograph Archive, London p. 124b; Salford Public Library p. 100b.

The Nichols Family Tree
(extract)

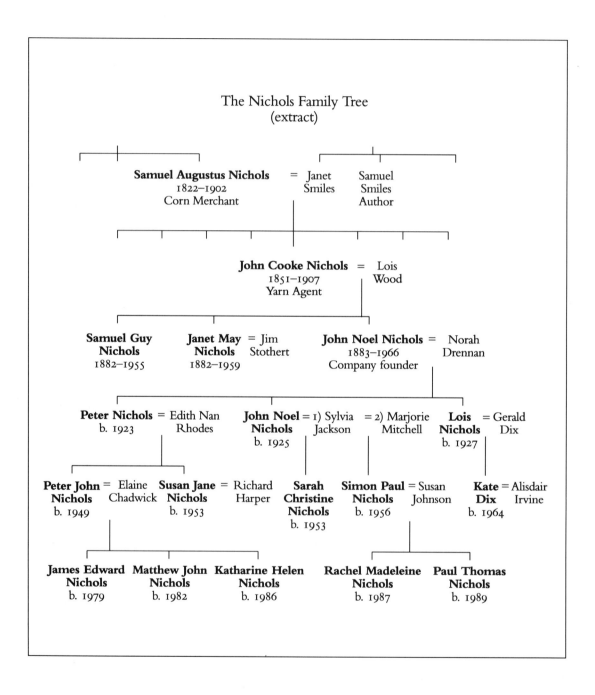

Samuel Augustus Nichols
1822–1902
Corn Merchant
= Janet
Smiles

Samuel
Smiles
Author

John Cooke Nichols = Lois
1851–1907   Wood
Yarn Agent

**Samuel Guy
Nichols**
1882–1955

**Janet May
Nichols**
1882–1959
= Jim
Stothert

John Noel Nichols = Norah
1883–1966   Drennan
Company founder

Peter Nichols = Edith Nan
b. 1923   Rhodes

**John Noel
Nichols**
b. 1925
= 1) Sylvia
Jackson
= 2) Marjorie
Mitchell

**Lois
Nichols**
b. 1927
= Gerald
Dix

**Peter John
Nichols**
b. 1949
= Elaine
Chadwick

**Susan Jane
Nichols**
b. 1953
= Richard
Harper

**Sarah
Christine
Nichols**
b. 1953

**Simon Paul
Nichols**
b. 1956
= Susan
Johnson

**Kate
Dix**
b. 1964
= Alisdair
Irvine

**James Edward
Nichols**
b. 1979

**Matthew John
Nichols**
b. 1982

**Katharine Helen
Nichols**
b. 1986

**Rachel Madeleine
Nichols**
b. 1987

**Paul Thomas
Nichols**
b. 1989

Preface

'VITALITY! VIVACITY! VIMTO!' proclaimed one of the more enthusiastic showcards in the 1950s. One could add the word 'versatility', for VIMTO is one of the most versatile drinks around. The entrepreneur John Noel Nichols hit upon a unique taste at the beginning of the century and it has been popular and familiar with four generations. The VIMTO name is an example of an old-established brand from a bygone era which has kept itself 'young' by adapting to changing tastes and conditions through its advertising and packaging. Characterised by a fun-loving, quality, healthy and good value image, VIMTO has found its appeal throughout its history from the gas-lit herbalist shop to consuming the canned drink on a street corner. Markets abroad, first reached in the 1920s, have shown the drink to have continuing international appeal.

The book is arranged according to the life cycle of the product, its origins and production, the advertising, how it has been packaged and where and why VIMTO is bought and consumed. Chapters on the export market and 'A Monument to VIMTO' are followed by some recipe ideas, some more bizarre than others.

My main primary source for this book has been the company archives which were stored haphazardly in boxes, safes, bottom drawers and cupboards. They consist of almost complete runs of catalogues, accounts and staff records. A small collection of orders and correspondence from bottling agents, herbalists and café owners was a useful source. Photographs and illustrations of the various business premises and of outlets and publicity events, both at home and abroad have been kept. Local history libraries and members of the public have kindly provided further illustrative material. The advertising of the brand is represented by a fine collection of showcards and promotional novelties which now form the VIMTO Advertising Collection.

Personal history is my second important source—either written or spoken. The Nichols family, members of staff and business associates have given information and impressions of the founder of the company and the workings and development of the business. Recollections of the past from many helpful people have given a nostalgic ambience to the drink and put it in its social context. I am always ready to hear more memories.

The VIMTO story is told to the present day so my viewpoint changes from that of a business, advertising and social historian to that of a contemporary observer. As the latter, it is difficult to be sure about what is significant or essential to the modern period. As a whole, I have had to be selective and personal interpretations and interests play a part. The views expressed are my own and not necessarily those of J. N. Nichols (Vimto) plc.

Sue Nichols, 1994

ABOVE. Noel Nichols in 1922, sitting in his first car, a Fiat 501 he bought in 1921. Before setting up his own business, Noel worked as a stockbroker's clerk and then as a soap factory manager and traveller. The grandnephew of the nineteenth-century exponent of 'Self Help', Samuel Smiles, he was a great believer in self-instruction, and continued to educate himself throughout his life, attending evening classes and doing correspondence courses.

LEFT. Bank House, Duke's Brow, Blackburn, in 1888. John Noel, the youngest of three children, was born here on 28 December 1883 to a yarn agent, John Cooke Nichols, and his wife Lois. The rambling seventeenth-century mansion still stands in its grounds. The small child in the picture could well be Noel Nichols, who was about five years old when this sketch was drawn by Charles Haworth for the book *Bits of Old Blackburn* (1889).

The Home of Vimto

SURROUNDED by the heady aroma of herbs, spices and essences from around the world, John Noel Nichols experimented with a wide range of flavoured fruit cordials, and finally devised a winning combination. He created a healthy pick-me-up 'tonic' which, it was claimed, would give those who drank it 'vim' and vigour. The year was 1908, and the concentrate was soon added to the list of goods which he supplied to the thriving herbalist shops and temperance bars in Manchester. The special flavour of the drink, along with its versatility, meant that it was a success from the beginning.

Early days

It was at 49 Granby Row, Manchester, that Noel Nichols set up his small business as a wholesale druggist and herb importer. As was common practice at the time, he was apparently financially backed by relatives. His brother Samuel and his brother-in-law Jim Stothert, a member of the family of wholesale druggists, each lent Noel Nichols £100. Buying in bulk, he would package a range of herbs, roots, spices and barks, along with colourings and flavourings, from which the herbalist could make up his or her own pills or medicated draughts. Ready-prepared goods such as nit ointment or camphor squares, together with pills and potions to

cope with a variety of ills, were also supplied. In addition, he also concocted a few speciality lines of his own, in the form of tonics.

In Britain, the service of doctors was provided free only to working men who made compulsory weekly contributions under the National Insurance Act, introduced by the Liberal government in 1911. For the majority of people, however, the cost of the visit and medicine was expensive. A collector would call each Friday night for the 6d. payment until the debt was paid off. Many people were taken to court if they could not pay. A remedy, and sometimes a cure, from the herbalist on the high street was often the first recourse—and the prices of the herbalist were often lower than those of the chemist.

Many herbalist shops had small areas for serving hot and cold tonic drinks and cordials. In addition, many towns had temperance bars which were set up specifically to sell non-alcoholic drinks. Individual owners, together with temperance and church groups, provided bars and meeting places such as billiard rooms as alternatives to pubs. They served mineral waters (as soft drinks were then called) and milk drinks instead of beers and spirits. J. N. Nichols and Company sold the ingredients for well-established drinks such as dandelion and burdock, sarsaparilla and herb beer. It also sold a powder called 'Thump', for milk drinks, which had but limited success—perhaps because of its name!

In 1908, the year in which VIMTO was invented, a Licensing Bill to restrict the long opening hours of public houses had been put to Parliament. In anticipation, *The Mineral Water Trade Review* of 1907, stated 'All manner of legislation for the encouragement of temperance is in the wind ... and this should be good news for the aerator'. The creation of a branded fancy drink concentrate for sale initially to herbalists and temperance bars, would, if it proved popular, help the rest of the business as other goods might be ordered at the same time. In that same auspicious year a sixteen-year-old family friend, Tom Broadhurst, joined Noel Nichols in his new venture. Tom's daughter, Ruth Kilby, recalls her father saying that Noel Nichols wanted to create a special non-alcoholic drink. They started by stirring several basic ingredients together in a barrel, and gradually put in a little more or less each time until the right balance of flavours was obtained. Noel Nichols would go round during the day on a bicycle taking orders. At night he would mix his cordial to the already secret recipe, then bottle and cork it ready for delivery the next day. Ernest Galley was another school leaver who helped on the production side. It appears that there were only three of them working to keep the small business going, coping with the buying of raw materials, production, packaging, advertising, selling, delivery and office work.

Success in Salford

As the business grew, the Granby Row office, factory and warehouse became too small, and in 1910 Noel Nichols moved to a rented building, 203A Chapel Street, in Salford. With good rail, canal and road connections, and the same soft water which was especially suitable for soft drink manufacture, a factory in Salford was well placed. Although Manchester was the first home of VIMTO, Salford is where the company became established and successful.

On 14 December 1912 the name "VIMTO" was registered as a trade mark in the 'Medicines' class and on 3 February 1913 was registered as a 'beverage for human use, not alcoholic, not aerated, and not medicated'. Although the description of a 'Health Tonic' which 'Keeps You Fit' was maintained until changes

Full of Vim !

Always merry and bright ! Full of energy and life ! A smile for everybody ! The will to win ! Dash and go that makes life good ! That is what VIMTO has done for him and that is what it can do for you.

VIMTO
The Ideal Beverage
is prepared from rare and delicious fruits, nuts, herbs and spices. You will feel the benefit from the very first glass.

Sold wherever mineral waters are obtainable, at usual high-class mineral water prices.

VIMTO gives VIM TO you

LEFT. Newspaper advertisement for VIMTO, 1929, extolling its marvellous effects.

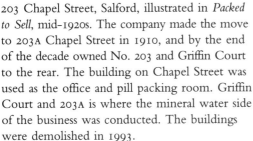

203 Chapel Street, Salford, illustrated in *Packed to Sell*, mid-1920s. The company made the move to 203A Chapel Street in 1910, and by the end of the decade owned No. 203 and Griffin Court to the rear. The building on Chapel Street was used as the office and pill packing room. Griffin Court and 203A is where the mineral water side of the business was conducted. The buildings were demolished in 1993.

Noel Nichols' wife, Norah, in the early 1920s.

in legislation after the Second World War, VIMTO cordial gradually became a soft drink to be taken for pleasure and the quenching of thirst. It was featured on the back page of the firm's much expanded catalogue and was described as 'Our Speciality'. As it was supplied in the form of an already sweetened concentrate, it was made up for the customer by the retailer simply by adding hot or cold water or soda water. The warning 'BEWARE of the many substitutes offered' showed that even

then the brand name and unique flavour had to be fiercely guarded. In 1915 Berni Brothers of Bargoed, mid-Glamorgan, were one of the first café proprietors to have a writ served upon them for selling an imitation red drink and calling it 'VIMTO'.

It was about the time of the move to Chapel Street that Noel Nichols began courting his future wife, Norah Drennan. They were cousins and had met again on holiday at their joint grandparents' family farm near Ancaster, Lincolnshire. Norah was a receptionist at the Great Western Hotel in Paddington, London. They married in March 1913, after which time Norah took an active part in the rapidly expanding firm, carrying out secretarial work, book-keeping and keeping staff records. The couple's first home was at 155 Ivy Road, a terraced house in Bolton.

At the beginning of the First World War, the staff had been increased to include two more travellers or salesmen, a secretary and two fourteen-year-old school leavers, one being Ted Lawton, who stayed with the firm to become foreman. A traveller's job was a hard one. Taking along samples and a catalogue, they would visit established customers and approach new businesses, tracking down bars and herbalist shops. Orders were taken, then deliveries were made by bicycle or trucks locally, or by rail nationally. Travellers were paid a salary, a commission on sales, and travelling expenses for hotels and transport either by rail, motor-bike or car depending on the seniority of the sales representative.

The order books from the year 1916 for the three salesmen, Mr Sydney Gray, Mr Thomas Baron and Noel Nichols himself, have survived. They show that VIMTO was sold to herbalists and temperance bars in the North West of England, North Wales and Yorkshire. Outlets in Glasgow and 'The Lancashire Temperance Bar' in Warminster, Wiltshire, were the only places outside the area. The records indicate that VIMTO concentrate was made to order at around 7s. a gallon, the exact price depending on the customer and the quantity. The company was determining the market price for the product and the catalogue entry for VIMTO reads 'prices upon application'.

In these pages of scrawled traveller's lists and written orders from customers there is a real feeling that one product, VIMTO, was really starting to take off. Mr Jackson, a herbalist on Entwistle Road, Blackburn, placed his

first order for the sixteen herbs and spices he needed in May 1916. As an afterthought he added 'I will give your VIMTO a trial and will you send me a showbill or two for it'. The order was quickly despatched and within a couple of days he wrote back 'I am more than pleased with your VIMTO. My customers have just raided me for it, and would you please send me another lot as this is ~~nearly~~ all done.' He crossed out the 'nearly' and added a postscript that as he was writing the letter he had sold the last drop. He also asked for another showbill as he had two windows, and presumably recognised the value of the advertising in drawing attention to the new product he was stocking.

The employment of new staff coincided with the Defence of the Realm Act (1915), which restricted licensing hours, increased excise duty and reduced the strength of alcoholic drinks. It was introduced in response to growing concern over public order, particularly in the armed forces. Key war industries such as munitions works, ship-building and transport were affected by bad time keeping due to the availability of cheap beers and spirits. The Act provided a boost for the growing mineral water trade, despite the war rationing of sugar.

The Vimto Agents

We know from company records that by 1921 concentrated VIMTO syrup had been adapted for the addition of carbonated water to make it up as an aerated or sparkling drink. The name "VIMTO" had been registered as a UK trade mark in the 'Mineral and Aerated

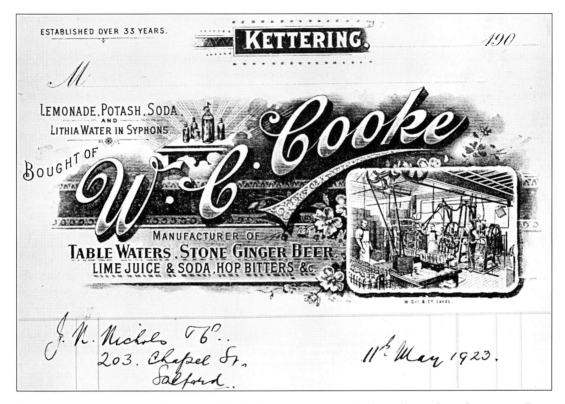

Letterhead of the VIMTO bottling agent, W. C. Cooke, depicting a bottling plant early in the century. By 1921 VIMTO concentrate was being sold in bulk to mineral water manufacturers in Britain and Ireland to bottle it in the carbonated form. It was packaged in a variety of bottles, with the unifying feature of the VIMTO label, supplied free of charge by the Nichols company. In the 1930s demand for VIMTO concentrate increased as agents improved their production capacity by installing new bottling lines.

Waters' class on 18 April 1919, in addition to the 'Medicines' and 'Cordials' classes. The Nichols Company did not bottle and carbonate VIMTO itself until 1969, when it acquired a bottling plant in Chorley. Instead, it appointed mineral water manufacturers as sole bottling agents in specific areas all over Great Britain and abroad. Between 1918 and 1925 a Sweetened Waters Excise Duty kept soft drink prices artificially high, so a higher price for a franchised 'speciality' or 'fancy' drink was more easily absorbed. Twelve-month contracts were signed under which the bottling agents agreed

to take a specific number of gallons of VIMTO concentrate each month at a set price. Sold in stoneware jars, glass carboys and wooden casks, the concentrate was transported by rail. Empty containers were returned for a refund, washing and re-use. Bottling agents nationwide were soon adding VIMTO to their range in response to advertisements in trade journals and local newspapers.

The bottlers would add carbonated water to the syrup then 'put it up', or package it, in a variety of bottle sizes and types depending on their bottling line. The Nichols Company supplied bottle body labels free of charge. Some firms had their delivery vans emblazoned with the name 'VIMTO' and the drink was given special prominence on their list of flavours. It had to be sold at a price set by the Nichols Company. Grocers, corner shops, cafés and cinemas all took bottles of sparkling VIMTO. Some bottlers also delivered a range of drinks direct to customers at home.

Many mineral water manufacturers had their own special flavours or versions of herbal drinks, but each order of VIMTO came with boxes of showcards and bottle display stands. If these were used they did not have to go to the expense of advertising their own products. Promotional gifts such as novelty postcards, the 'VIMTO Book', and bottle openers, were also much in demand and encouraged the bottler to re-order.

Bottling agents who did not fulfil their agreement of ordering certain quantities of VIMTO were chased up and told that their agency rights would be taken away from them. A bundle of letters giving a variety of reasons for low sales gives an insight as to how VIMTO was regarded within the trade. T. Baker from Woodford, London, wrote in April 1924 that 'there has not been a huge demand for non-alcoholic beverages recently' but still wished to continue his agency. Thomson and Sons in Barrow-in-Furness, writing in October 1926, said that VIMTO was not selling well through no fault of the goods but because there was 'a great shortage of money in the district and the Coal Strike and the Winter'. Kinmond & Co. of Leamington wrote in March 1924 that sales were difficult as 'this town is purely a residential place with

only about one third of the population being of the artisan class, likely to purchase this class of drink'. They were also competing against an already established drink called 'Valento', which has now long gone.

On a more positive note, the bottlers who found VIMTO a 'good business maker' were asked in 1926 to give 'Testimonials' on the drink, which could be used in trial order form, leaflets and later the give-away diaries. Ralph Bell of Wakefield declared ' "VIMTO" has proved itself to be unlike other "speciality beverages". Folk don't get tired of it, they drink it all the year round.' Forster, Coverdale and Company of York and Scarborough declared 'It is a splendid trade getter, because it seems to us that people must talk of it to their friends. They in turn ask for it from their shop keeper who is "compelled" to stock it.' New business was thus created by consumer demand. Hunt and Horsfield of Halifax also talked of the public's reaction in June 1926: 'It is certainly appreciated by the public, some have even praised its medicinal properties besides being an ideal thirst quencher'.

Ayres Road, Old Trafford

By 1926 VIMTO cordial was being bottled by Nichols initially for sale through herbalists to the public, who were thus able to make drinks for themselves at home. This was probably prompted by the reduction in the price of sugar in 1925. The cordial was available in dark green bottles with a black and white label captioned 'Builds up the System'. With a rapidly growing demand for the cordial and

VIMTO cordial appears alongside other herbal remedies in the *Packed to Sell* catalogue, 1926. VIMTO cordial was not available in bottles for sale to the public until 1926. It took its place amongst the company's other packaged pills, potions and tonics as a healthy tonic which 'builds up the system'.

the VIMTO compound (as it was now described) both at home and abroad, the Chapel Street premises were proving too small. A new home for VIMTO was therefore found in the Old Trafford area of Manchester, in 1927. The Britannia Laundry building in Brooks' Bar had been built soon after the Boer War and had a tall chimney originally for the large water heating boiler. The VIMTO name soon appeared painted on the chimney bricks and later on a wind sock flying from a mast. It was situated at Ayres Road and occupied the whole block between Milner Street and Powell Street. Some of the staff lived within walking distance of the factory or had children at the nearby school. By the end of the decade an average of thirty-two people were employed, half of whom had been with the firm since the early 1920s or before.

Most of the staff who were eligible joined the company's newly formed 'thrift' or pension scheme in 1929. Those who were over twenty-one and had been in service for over twelve months could join, with the company matching the employee's payment of a few shillings a week towards his or her retirement income.

The internal appearance of the office remained unchanged well into the 1950s as Mrs Marion Hughes (née Kirby) remembers when she joined the firm as an office junior as late as 1959. 'On a wintry February morning I remember entering the old office building and feeling as if I'd been transplanted back in time to a Charles Dickens story, with the old fashioned high wooden desks with their upright seats in front of the windows. To my left was a tiled fireplace with a lovely warm fire.' Most of the staff had been there for thirty years or more and, seeing she was nervous, chatted to her and made her feel at home. 'It was like belonging to one big happy family working in the office,' she recalls. Doreen Dean (née Litler), who had joined the firm in 1944, remembers one hazard. 'When you had short legs you had a heck of a job getting up onto those high stools! And just as you had got settled the telephone would ring.'

Norah Nichols had worked for the company in the office until the birth of her first child, Peter, in 1923. The couple had two more children, John Noel—named after his father—and Lois. They often came into the office to see the staff and look around the factory. Mrs Nichols' mother's help, Alice Turner (née Townsend) was known as Miss 'T'. The family home was a large detached house called The Homestead on Light Oaks Road, Pendleton near Salford. Mr Nichols was driven to work by his chauffeur, Jack Beaman.

The children of John Noel Nichols—
from left to right, Lois, John and Peter—on holiday in Scarborough, 1931.

Further Expansion

The company was incorporated in September 1929 and renamed J. N. Nichols and Company Ltd. The majority of the shares were held by Noel Nichols. With a much larger production capacity for VIMTO concentrate, the late 1920s also saw a new drive to attract more agents to bottle VIMTO both at home and abroad. Adverts in the local papers almost implied that it was their moral duty to bottle it as the local population was desperate to buy it. Caterers and shopkeepers were also advised to 'Look out for the "VIMTO" man!' : 'Swansea wants "VIMTO"!' was a typical advert in a local newspaper. The VIMTO pocket diary made its appearance in 1929. Through the 1930s it was filled with exhortation and encouragement, using phrases such as 'If you have the "plant" we have the

"Drink" to make it grow' or 'Why sell American drinks when there is "VIMTO".' Mineral water companies were discouraged from experimenting with new flavours, on the grounds that there was already VIMTO, which had proved popular, successful and profitable for over twenty years. The diary also thanked the customers for adhering strictly to the bottling and serving instructions, thus maintaining a high reputation and 'retaining the elusive but fascinating flavour of "VIMTO" which the public likes so well'. Even so, a few more bottlers would top up the VIMTO compound with cheaper ingredients such as Cherryade, doing a disservice both to the VIMTO taste and to the honest bottlers.

In 1932 VIMTO cordial was offered for sale to bottlers to sell alongside the sparkling product to retailers. They were encouraged to push

VIMTO cordial sales for hot drinks during the winter months when sales of carbonated drinks were lower and their staff not as busy. It was suggested that it helped their sales as it made the public even more aware of VIMTO. A publicity campaign in London, in the form of newspaper advertisements and leaflets, announced that it was now obtainable at Selfridges, Fortnum and Masons and Harrods. It was now sold in three sizes at fixed prices to the customer of 2s. 6d., 1s. 6d. and the new 10d. size, and came in a clear glass bottle embossed with flowers and leaves. A new label had also been introduced to match the more 'modern' carbonated VIMTO label which had also been changed in 1928.

The VIMTO flavour had also been put on the market in the form of pastilles, a milk shake syrup and an ice-cream topping .

The Eve of War

In 1938, Joe Pearson, whom Noel Nichols had known as a child, joined the firm. After training for five years at the Manchester Municipal College of Technology (now UMIST), near VIMTO's first home, Joe became the chief chemist. He became works manager in 1961, when Tom Broadhurst, the first employee of the company, retired at the age of seventy. Joe became a director and retired in 1985.

In 1939 Noel Nichols' eldest son, Peter, joined the company straight from school at the age of sixteen. He started working in the factory weighing out the herbs, roots and barks by the pound into paper bags for the herbalist shops. He also packed the bottles of cordial for export into wooden cases.

With the outbreak of war, Peter Nichols and many of the sales staff joined the forces. Two of the travellers' wives, Mrs Gray and Mrs Hardy, did some selling while their husbands were away. The night-time fire watch on the factory was done by pairs on a rota basis. On the night Manchester was blitzed in October 1941 Peter Nichols recalls incendiary bombs coming through the glass roof in showers. Luckily the floor was made of concrete and all the fires were extinguished with stirrup pumps kept on the premises. An air-raid shelter had been bought in March 1940 at a cost of £162 14s. 6d.

The soft drinks industry at war

For part of the war the Nichols company continued in business but in disguise. In conjunction with the trade, The Soft Drinks Industry (War Time) Association Ltd (SDI) was formed by the Ministry of Food in order to concentrate and organise the manufacture and distribution of soft drinks. From 1942 to 1948 small businesses were forced to close and the larger ones were strictly controlled. All labour and supplies needed by the firm, including raw materials, bottles and petrol for transport, were recorded and the output of the finished product monitored. The flavour and ingredients of the cordials, squashes and mineral waters were made to a Government formulation. Manufacturers who had previously made a particularly local drink and who had raw materials in stock could continue production under the name 'Speciality Flavour Cordial.' Although brand names were not allowed, VIMTO appeared under the

A still photograph from Paul Rotha's visionary wartime film on food production and distribution, *World of Plenty*, 1945. Women queue outside Elliott's grocers for rationed food. They no longer have a wide choice of branded products such as VIMTO, which nevertheless are still advertised in the window.

guise of a 'SFC' and most local customers realised that they were really buying their favourite drink. A code replaced the company or brand name and simple, standardised labels were issued. Pricing was also fixed and competition eliminated. These moves were made to protect the market share of the smaller companies which had been temporarily closed. The small profits made by the larger companies were shared by those who had been forced to close. The overall quality of the drinks was poor, however, due to the restrictions on the ingredients, particularly sugar. The sweetness was given mainly by saccharin, with sugar reduced to 20 per cent of the pre-war levels. The public came to accept the products of the SDI, though cynics suggested that the initials stood for 'Some Die Instantly'.

Although there was a shortage of newsprint and paper, and advertising was heavily restricted, small advertisements for VIMTO appeared regularly in newspapers throughout the war, even though the branded product could not be bought. The firm's small contribution to boost the nation's morale included captions such as

'Speed on Victory and the return of "VIMTO" too.' After a sixteen-week de-concentration period from October 1947, the regulations were lifted, and trademarks and more extensive advertising reappeared. VIMTO was one of the few branded soft drinks to have survived the war, no doubt because of the newspaper advertising and the red enamelled advertisements which had been sported by many outlets since the late '30s. By December 1947, Rider Wilson's Table Waters in Sheffield put an advertisement in the local press announcing ' "VIMTO"; the famous drink is on sale again in split bottles. The demand will be great but supplies are limited', and suggested that, as they were the authorised local bottlers, they would have a regular supply. This shortage continued until 1953 when sugar was finally de-rationed, and bottles were in greater supply.

After the war

Many of the smaller mineral water manufacturers, particularly in the south of England, did not set up business again after the war. It was at that time that the market for VIMTO in that area was lost, as it was the sparkling version, which was distributed by bottlers which had mainly been sold, rather than the cordial. As with countries abroad, it was more economical to send concentrate in bulk to bottlers to add carbonated water, rather than transport bottles of cordial for resale. The larger companies such as Nichols, which had continued production during the war, began to modernise and mechanise for large-scale manufacture. New stainless steel vats, fillers and labelling machines were purchased.

Newspaper advertisement, April 1944.

Pre-war advertising of the cordial had been mainly restricted to the winter months, as the works was busy producing concentrate for sparkling VIMTO packaged by bottling agents during the summer period. Now that the production capacity for the bottling of cordial at Ayres Road had improved, it too was promoted vigorously throughout the year.

The ice-cream powder and herbalist side of the business did not, however, modernise its production techniques. These are evocatively described by Mrs J. A. Bluer (née Dutton), who came to work with the company as a school-leaver from 1946 to 1950:

Near to our room—grandly called the 'Manufacturing Chemist Department'—was a very small room wherein worked an old lady packing cornflour and custard powder. Sometimes, in the winter, we would fancy something hot at lunch time to warm us up. Gladys, the forelady, would send me across the road to a dairy for a pint of milk; then, to go upstairs to the stove and make us all some cups of custard. We used to sit around with our feet in boxes full of shredded paper, each with a cup of hot creamy custard. We soon warmed up, and I can honestly say that I have never since tasted custard so nice.

The people in the dairy where I went for the milk always commented on how I smelled so sweetly whenever I went there. It must have been a combination of aromas from the various herbs and fruit juice concentrates clinging to my clothes.

Modern day production methods had no place in our Manufacturing Chemist Department. Just at the side of the room with the Custard Powder Lady was an even smaller room where we produced liquorice 'Imps'. Sheets of liquorice were passed through a hand-turned machine something like a smaller version of a washday mangle, except that these rollers were deeply engraved with a cross-cross scoring which impressed into the sheets a pattern of tiny squares. These patterned sheets were then put onto trays to set hard overnight. Next day we would break the hardened sheets into pieces which were then placed into a canvas bag. Having tied the bag securely, we then proceeded to pound it with a heavy wooden mallet until all the pieces had shattered and become individual 'Imps'. These were then weighed and boxed ready for sale. Them were the days!

Because of the implementation of the National Health Service Act in 1948, free prescriptions and medical advice meant that the herbalists soon lost their prominence. The sale of herbs, pills, powders and potions by the Nichols' company also gradually ceased,

Gladys, the Forelady, and her assistant, Margaret, in the 'Manufacturing Chemist Department' Ayres Road, *c*.1948.

with soft drinks becoming the mainstay of the company and VIMTO as the main brand. A trade advertisement in 1956 gave three cast-iron reasons why the retailer should stock up with VIMTO cordial: 'The name is well-known and trusted, the product is of fine quality, and you've been backed by national advertising.' This was the year of the first VIMTO television commercial. Fred Holt became the advertising representative for the North West region, delivering VIMTO showcards and novelties and maintaining the pre-war red enamelled signs.

The three children of John Noel—Lois Dix, John and Peter—at the opening of the VIMTO exhibition at Quarry Bank Mill, Styal, 1991.

'Mr Peter' started to learn the office work and did a Business Studies course. He was made a director in 1947 and gradually took over the running of the company from his father. Lois Nichols (later Mrs Gerald Dix) also worked for the firm in the late 1940s and early '50s with chief chemist Joe Pearson before training as a horticulturist in Reading. With her experience of packaging apples, she introduced to the firm the idea of pallets as a way of moving heavy boxes efficiently.

'Mr John' joined the firm in 1950, having served in the RAF and then obtaining a degree in Commerce. At first he was a traveller in the Lancashire cotton towns, accompanying Bill Lee, an experienced salesman. He was also involved in the tracking down of VIMTO imitations. Throughout VIMTO's history, poor copies have been attempted or the name used fraudulently. John Nichols junior remembers the procedure for catching café owners who would sell a red fruity drink under the VIMTO name. Two members of staff would go to the bar and ask for a glass of VIMTO, confirming that it was VIMTO when it was made for them. They would sit down, taste it, and if it was deemed to be a cheap imitation, they would produce two bottles from a briefcase. The so-called 'VIMTO' would be poured into each bottle and labelled with the date and name of the café. The owner was given one bottle and told that he had better keep it as his evidence as he would most likely be prosecuted for claiming to be selling VIMTO when he was actually selling an imitation product. More often than not an apology would be published in newspapers of Nichols' choosing, with all costs paid by the offending and embarrassed café owner. 'Mr John' also assisted Harold Hughes on the export side of the business which was expanded in the mid-1950s. He took over the Middle East market and was appointed a director in 1957.

A growing industry

The enormous expansion of soft drinks sales in Britain in the 1950s continued into the next decade. The particularly good summer of 1959 and the competition from American soft drinks saw a rationalisation of the industry. Trade was consolidated into a smaller number of larger units to take advantage of national distribution and advertising on television and in the newspapers. The new 'teenage' generation were large-scale consumers of soft drinks and the industry seemed set for expansion, as it was hoped that the habit would persist in later life. There was also indirect promotion of soft drinks through the 'safe driving' campaigns, though the health risks of alcohol were yet to be well publicised. In April 1962 the Government tapped the increasing success of the industry by levying a purchase tax of 15 per cent on the wholesale price of soft drinks, sweets and ice cream. It was seen as a tax on children, but despite the outcry, it was soon absorbed as the market grew.

As a product with a strong brand loyalty and reputation for quality and good value VIMTO was well able to compete in the growing market for soft drinks. It was versatile, covering both the 'dilute to taste' sector, whether hot or cold, and the carbonates consumed either as an individual drink or to lesser extent as a mixer. This versatility meant that it could be marketed in different ways. Unlike the various colas and orange drinks on the market, VIMTO has a unique and original flavour.

On 16 February 1961, J. N. Nichols and Company Limited changed its name to J. N. Nichols (VIMTO) Limited when it became a public company. The shares were placed and quoted on the Manchester Stock Exchange by Henry Cooke, Lumsden and priced at 9s. They opened on the day at 11s. 4½d. and closed at 12s. 1½d, having had favourable tips in the financial press. At that time, the Directors and Nichols family held 69½ per cent of the share capital. The staff were encouraged to purchase shares at the preferential price of 9s. If they had bought 100 shares at £45 at the time they would now, at time of writing, have 3,000 shares, due to share splits, worth over £6,600. The value of the shares has gone up twelve times more than the Retail Price Index. Some

of the staff who bought shares are now retired but still keep in touch by coming along to the Annual General Meeting, including 'the two Eileens'—Eileen Brocklehurst and Eileen Hudson—Brian Kilby, Bill Lee, Joe Pearson and Marjorie Stevenson.

At the time of the flotation, a useful advertisement was published giving the public some information about the company, which was described as the 'Proprietors of "VIMTO" the popular speciality Soft Drink'. The company had sixty employees including clerical staff and sales representatives. Noel Nichols was seventy-seven years old and described as 'actively engaged in the business all his working life'. The company's plant for washing, bottling and labelling of the cordial had been gradually fully mechanised and further machinery which was on order would speed up the process.

Mr Nichols senior continued to come into the office every day from his home in Hale Barns, Cheshire, taking an active interest in the running of the company. In 1964 he became president and technical director, whilst his sons Peter and John became joint managing directors. He died in August 1966 at the age of eighty-two, his wife Norah having died seven years earlier. In his will he left money to all the long-serving employees. He had previously given the farm land behind their house Prestwood, Hale Barns, for the grounds of the Hale Barns Cricket Club, in perpetuity. He had seen his business grow from a small office and warehouse, dependent on orders of single bottles of VIMTO concentrate or a few camphor squares, to a company selling millions of gallons of VIMTO across the world. His invention had held favour with the public for fifty-eight

The cordial bottling line at the Wythenshawe plant, installed in 1993. The grape, blackcurrant and raspberry juices and other (secret) ingredients are mixed with liquid sugar in stainless steel vats. The cordial is then piped to the bottling line where the 725ml glass bottles or 1.5 litre PET bottles are rinsed and filled. The caps and labels are swiftly applied, the bottles collated on a cardboard tray, shrink wrapped and palletised automatically.

years and had never stopped growing in popularity. He would have been aware of the growing trends in soft drinks to come as already revealed by the American market. Supermarket sales, new forms of packaging, vending machines, draught soft drinks and low calorie products were all to change what had been, in essence, a nineteenth-century industry.

New forms of advertising, including colour television, glossy magazines and label promotions, were also on the horizon. It was left to his sons to continue to expand and modernise the company, and to his grandsons to take it towards the twenty-first century.

The move to Wythenshawe

With the general growth of the soft drinks industry, the Nichols company has continued to expand. The production line at the Ayres Road factory, where 1,000 bottles of cordial a day were filled, proved too small. In 1970 it was decided that a new works and offices were essential to meet the ever-increasing demand. At the new Roundthorn Industrial Estate on Ledson Road in Wythenshawe, South Manchester, a purpose-built factory was completed in 1971. Both the office and warehouse space have subsequently been further expanded. In 1992, a new syrup pasteuriser, laboratory suite and quality control area were installed. The following year, two high-speed bottling lines were purchased to increase production capacity to meet growing demand. The integrated rinsing, filling, capping, labelling, tray and shrink-wrapping and palletising functions are fully automatic.

The third generation

By 1966 all three of Noel Nichols' offspring had married and now had families of their own. Peter John and Jane are Peter Nichols' children, Sarah and Simon are John Nichols' and Kate is Lois Dix's daughter. Like their parents before them, the children were often

Gary Unsworth (Business Development Director), Simon Nichols (Finance Director) and John Nichols (Managing Director) at the Wythenshawe office, 1993.

brought into the Ayres Road office and factory to say 'hello' to the staff.

The three grand-daughters have made successful careers outside the firm. Jane Harper is a dietician, Sarah Nichols is a curator of Decorative Arts at the Carnegie Institute in Pittsburgh and Kate Irvine, after a period in an advertising agency, now designs and makes her own jewellery.

As was the tradition at the time, the two male grandchildren, Peter John and Simon, joined the firm and gradually took over the running of the company. Peter John, who has always been called John, joined the firm in 1971 as a Combined Sciences graduate. He became production manager and a director in 1975. In 1982 he was appointed sales and marketing director, becoming group managing director in 1986 on the retirement of his father, Peter Nichols. Simon Nichols joined the firm in 1983, as a chartered accountant with a degree in Business Administration. He

VIMTO lorry, 1994, with the livery based on the scripted logo and fruit imagery found on the packaging of the sparkling version of the product.

worked alongside the financial director and company secretary, Brian Kilby. Brian, another chartered accountant, is the son-in-law of Tom Broadhurst, who was the company's first employee in 1908. Simon joined the board in 1986 and became financial director and company secretary at the retirement of Brian Kilby in 1988. John Nichols junior, Simon's father, had retired in 1985.

As with any other large business today, recruitment of staff is no longer mainly dependent on contacts with friends or relations, as it was in the past. People who are already qualified and experienced join the firm, rather than starting as office juniors and working their way up. The company employs 250 people throughout the group, and although the main types of work are the same as in the past—production, office work and selling—the days of mixing in a wooden barrel or the ledger written in pen and ink are long gone. The staff are now helped by highly automated machinery in the factories and the latest integrated computer systems in the office. As in former times, however, staff turnover is very low and a friendly family atmosphere is maintained.

The days of the individual sales representative personally taking orders from a grocer for a few bottles of VIMTO, to be delivered by a small van a week or so later, have also disappeared.

The role of the salesperson has changed. When a new product is launched, the skills of communication and persuasion are relied upon, although coverage in the trade press has also become very important. In terms of day-to-day sales however, the sales people simply need to deliver promotional material and check on stocks of Nichols' products, advising cash and carry warehouse managers when a new order should be placed. Increasingly, orders by-pass humans and are sent directly through computers, from the central supermarket warehouses or cash and carry depots in response to their own stock control systems at the cash register, to the VIMTO distribution warehouse at Haydock, Merseyside.

A fleet of lorries emblazoned with the VIMTO name makes the deliveries.

The board of directors also has a greater diversity, reflecting the public company status, which means that they are responsible to major institutional shareholders as well as a loyal band of individuals. The Nichols family still retain around 30 per cent of the share capital.

The secret recipe

The recipe for VIMTO has changed little from Noel Nichols' original creation. Only two people know the full list of about twenty-nine ingredients (no one will tell me the exact number), and their proportions. Some of its many and varied ingredients include raspberry, blackcurrant and grape juices, vanilla, capsicum and the herb horehound. The artificial colours have been replaced by natural colours and a healthy serving of vitamin C has also been added to the drink. The product now contains a higher proportion of fruit juice than when it was first formulated. The original taste, however, has been carefully maintained. These changes were made in response to consumer demand, and a media advertising campaign informed the public of the improvements.

Vimto in Cans

VIMTO was first produced and sold in steel cans in Britain in about 1964 by Stotherts Ltd, who had sole canning rights: a member of this family had helped Noel Nichols set up his business in 1908. In 1980 Solent Canners in Southampton was acquired, and in 1982 the Nichols company was thus able to begin to can VIMTO itself, after

an agreement had been reached with A. G. Barr plc, who had taken over Stotherts Ltd. In addition to the home market, Solent Canners primarily supplied the Middle East market, which previously only had access to VIMTO cordial. The canned 'pin hi' range came with the company. The factory also carries out contract canning for other soft drink companies such the ubiquitous Coca-Cola. In 1987, a new canning line was installed at Solent at a cost of £2 million. Cans are filled at the amazing rate of sixteen a second.

The sale of single cans in supermarkets is being replaced by multi-packaging, a process which is also undertaken at Solent Canners. Single chilled can sales are mainly available in cabinets in cafés and small grocery shops or by vending machines. These methods ensure that drinks are well displayed and sold under optimum conditions.

Sparkling Vimto

Wherever VIMTO is bottled or canned in the world, the process uses only the original concentrate, which is made by the Nichols company nowhere else except at the Wythenshawe factory. This ensures that the quality and contents of the secret recipe remain strictly under the company's control. Over fifty thriving franchise companies, mainly in the Midlands, the north of England and Scotland, still bottle sparkling VIMTO. As in the past, they distribute directly to corner shops, independent grocers, cafés and pubs. Door-to-door deliveries are also still made by a few bottling agents and in conjunction with milk supplies.

In 1969, for the first time, the Nichols company was able to carbonate and bottle

VIMTO in its own plant. The old established firm of T. & R. Smith in Chorley, Lancashire, was acquired, along with its branded 'Sunglora' range of soft drinks. The factory was eventually closed in 1990, and in that year the bottling plant of William Morgan (Bryn) at Haydock was purchased, together with the surrounding land.

Experiencing the Vimto taste

Since the early 1980s ready-to-drink VIMTO has been available in the popular Tetra Brik and plastic cup form. These are filled by Healds Juices and Calypso Soft Drinks respectively, who are sent VIMTO concentrate in 1,000-litre square metal containers from the Wythenshawe factory. VIMTO has been sold under licence in other forms. The popular 'Jubbly' tetrahedron pack of the 1950s was packaged by Calypso Soft Drinks and frozen by shopkeepers. It provided a refreshing iced lolly with a trickle of VIMTO cordial to finish off with. The elongated iced lolly in sealed foil wrapping, the 'freeze-drink', is its modern-day equivalent. VIMTO ice lollies on a stick are also produced by other ice cream manufacturers. The VIMTO pastille has long gone, but the VIMTO lollipop is still a favourite.

'Diet' and 'Low Sugar' versions

Apart from the new forms of packaging and point-of-sale areas, the major change for the VIMTO range was the introduction of a sparkling 'Diet' version in the spring of 1987. At first, in the 1970s, low-calorie drinks were perceived as being 'feminine' and 'southern'. However, now that there is a generally more health-conscious nation, concerned with levels of sugar consumption, the demand for 'diet' VIMTO has widened. The diet drink is now considered 'unisex' and suitable for those who are weight-conscious but not necessarily on a diet. Dental care is also a consideration. The introduction of more versatile artificial sweeteners with a negligible after-taste and good shelf-life sealed the future of diet drinks. The sparkling version of VIMTO sweetened with 'Sunett' was an immediate success, achieving a 25 per cent increase in canned drink sales during the first year. A 'Low Sugar' VIMTO cordial was successfully launched in 1993 with a cry of 'at last' from calorie conscious VIMTO cordial fans.

Other flavours

Apart from VIMTO, the company also produces a variety of other drinks. Popular flavours such as a cola, orange and shandy came under the 'pin-hi' title—the name being a golfing term—which was acquired along with Solent Canners. 'Orange Plus' with extract of ginseng root follows on in the herbal tradition, while novelty drinks such as the bubble-gum flavoured 'Hubba Bubba' are also popular. The tropical 'Bali-Hi' and the unusual 'Matotaki' with sake flavouring are two other drinks in the range. The topical Russian peppermint and ginger drink, 'МИР', pronounced 'mir' meaning 'world peace', has come and gone. After many years 'Sarsaparilla' has been dropped, much to the dismay of the few remaining keen drinkers.

Promotional leaflet for the Ginseng range,
1993. 'Lemon Plus' with extract of ginseng root
was introduced in 1992 after the success of
'Orange Plus' with extract of ginseng root.

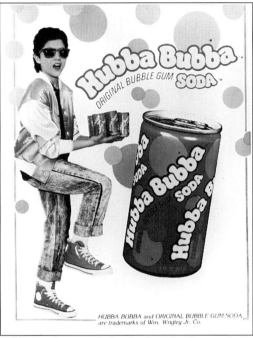

Publicity photograph for the launch of canned
'Hubba Bubba', 1991. Novelty drinks made
under licence by J. N. Nichols (VIMTO) plc, such
as this lurid pink liquid, continue to sell well.

Vending

Vending machines provide instant drinks in
various ways—by providing a can, by adding
hot water to powders for tea, coffee, hot
chocolate or soup, or by adding cold water
to concentrated syrups to make a cool drink.
With its use nationwide in the Vendops Ltd
machines from 1981, VIMTO showed its versatility, being dispensed as a hot or cold drink.

Independent Vending Supplies Ltd was a
successful Skelmersdale company started by
two brothers, Gary and Ian Unsworth, and it
supplied ingredients for vending machines. In
1986 J. N. Nichols (VIMTO) plc acquired the
company. Coffee, chocolate and other drinks
are supplied to the leisure and catering trade
and the name was changed to Nichols Foods
Ltd in 1988. The company was the first
brand-based vending ingredients firm to be
awarded the BS5750 Part II quality assurance
certificate, in 1990. Gary Unsworth became
a director of the parent company in 1992.

Can-vending machines of the latest design,
featuring VIMTO and other Nichols' products,
are now being sold or rented to the vendors'
trade. The current trend in vending is to have
two machines—a hot drinks dispenser and an
accompanying chilled can machine. It is a far

cry from the dark and aromatic days of the herbalist shop, although the desire of people for a warming drink in winter and a thirst-quenching soft drink in summer remains much the same.

Post-mix

An extension of the concept of the soda fountain, which had featured so prominently in temperance bars, was the draught vending system whereby the addition of water and carbon dioxide to a concentrate is done simultaneously, either over the counter or on a self-service basis.

From 1982 VIMTO concentrate was supplied to Cabana Soft Drinks, Preston, for sale in licensed outlets, clubs, leisure centres, hospitals and schools, and in 1986 Cabana was acquired by the Nichols company. Apart from the addition of sparkling mineral water or soda water, it was also possible to produce fizzy VIMTO economically in the home since the Sodastream Company added it to their range in 1982.

New systems

This great variety of soft drinks in their various forms of packaging is mainly collected together at the new distribution warehouse, which was built in the grounds of the Haydock bottling plant in 1991. Bottles of cordial from Wythenshawe, cans from Southampton, Tetra Briks from Manchester, cups from Tattenhall and bottles of carbonated drinks from Haydock are arranged by the pallet load on enormous shelves with rollers called a 'live racking system'. Some stocks are also held at Solent Canners in Southampton for southern distribution. At the time of writing, a new factory, office and warehouse is under construction on the Haydock site. Nichols Foods will move here from Skelmersdale to take advantage of economies of scale.

The future

The soft drinks industry is still a rapidly growing market, with consumption in the UK more than doubling since 1979. This growth is partly due to changing lifestyles which have coincided with the fast-food boom. An awareness of the possible dangers of alcohol, and an increasingly health-conscious attitude on the part of the consumer, have resulted in the phenomenal rise in sales of mineral waters, low-calorie and low-sugar drinks, and fruit-juice based products in particular. VIMTO's share of the market is growing more rapidly than the increase in the market itself.

The market has also seen polarisation between the two big monopolistic 'cola kings'—Pepsi-Cola and Coca-Cola. The role of the independent producer with unique branded products has become even more important if consumer choice is to be maintained. The Nichols company is well placed to accept this challenge and see its chief product, VIMTO, through to its centenary birthday party in 2008. By that time it may be the fourth generation of Nichols—James, Matthew, Katharine, Rachel and Paul—who will be organising the celebrations.

The Temperance Movement in the 20th Century

Street theatre produced by the Smith Street Temperance, probably Ordsall, in the early 1920s.

The temperance movement began in Lancashire in the 1830s in response to the waste and misery caused by what was termed 'the demon drink'. It campaigned through plays, lectures and grand marches, as well as by leaflets, song books and promotional novelties such as mugs and even wallpaper. The most often used subjects for plays and lantern shows was that of the father beating his impoverished wife and children, having spent their only income at the pub, which was sadly true to life.

Pledge card and leaflet published by the British (National) Temperance League, Sheffield, in the 1920s.

Many prominent figures, including King George V and Don Bradman, took the pledge, but the movement had difficulty in competing against the advertising campaigns of the brewers.

Drink to me only with thine
eyes—
And I will pledge with
VIMTO

LEFT. **Illustration taken from the *New Vimto Book for Scholars*, late 1920s.**
VIMTO was created as a temperance drink and the bottle labels described it as non-alcoholic well into the 1960s. This illustration shows a man in love taking the pledge with VIMTO.

BELOW. Despite this alliance with the anti-alcohol campaign, VIMTO is regarded by many as an excellent mixer for alcoholic drinks. Between the wars the company itself promoted the mixing of VIMTO with whisky, stout and rum. This is a showcard from the 1920s.

ASK FOR A WHISKY AND
"VIMTO"
MOST DELIGHTFUL

The Action Props Manager of Granada TV's *Prime Suspect III* in 1993 preparing a bottle of 'Burgundy' from Vimto cordial!
Many an actor has remained sober on stage or on a film set by sipping VIMTO rather than red wine or port. It is also sometimes used as Communion 'wine'.

Remedies from the Herbalist

A hebalist selects some senna leaves, 1920s. Before the introduction of free health care in the late 1940s, the final recourse for many ill people was a remedy—and occasionally a cure—from a herbalist on the high street. The Nichols company gradually extended its range of imported herbs, roots and barks, along with the colourings and flavourings from which the herbalist could make up pills and medicated draughts.

'The herbalist shops played a very important role in the community in those days. No other shops were open on Sundays, so we used to congregate around, or inside, the herbalist's. We would look at all the jars and bottles of dried leaves, flowers sticks and different powders. We used to ask the herbalist what they were for, and he would tell us. When I got older I would have to go for different items for our family, and go errands for other people in the street.'

Albert Heaviside on a herbalist shop in Miles Platting in the 1920s (1991).

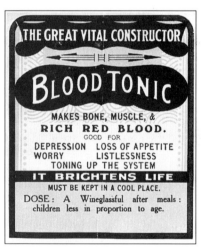

A label for 'The Great Vital Constructor Blood Tonic', 1920s. This is one example of dubious advertising made before stricter controls on the claims made for such tonics were introduced in 1936.

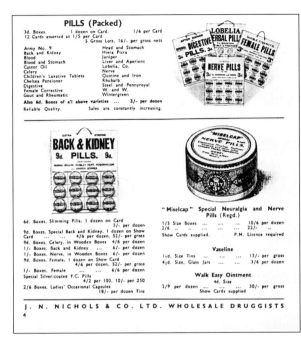

The Packed Goods catalogue, mid-1920s (detail).

The company also bought goods in bulk from the large manufacturers and packaged them down into small quantities for sale to herbalists and corner shops. Pills, powders, ointments, dried herb combinations and concentrated mixtures described as 'Packed Goods, smartly put up and all quick selling lines' were sold in great variety in the 1920s and 30s. In recent times there has been a revival of herbal remedies, with growing concern over the side-effects of some modern drugs.

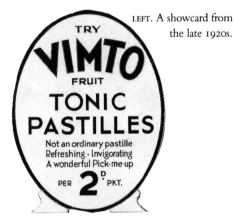

LEFT. A showcard from the late 1920s.

BELOW. **Showcard from the early 1920s.**
The company bought the syrup in bulk and bottled it by hand with a funnel.

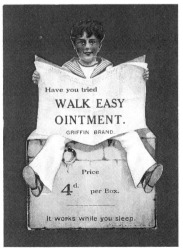

A showcard for 'Walk Easy Ointment', early 1920s.

Ayres Road

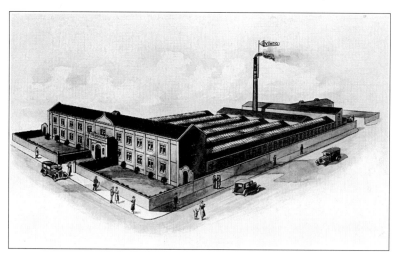

An idealised view of the Britannia works and offices on Ayres Road, Old Trafford, 1935 (gouache).
In 1927 the company moved to the former Britannia Laundry building. The main office was on the ground floor at the front, with the factory, garages and warehouse for the fleet of transport vehicles at the rear. The children from the nearby school used to play in the garden.

Miss Smethurst, the office manager, at the front entrance to the Ayres Road works, 1928.
She holds a bottle of sparkling VIMTO and is accompanied by two bottle shields which were carried to advertise VIMTO on the streets.

The office, Ayres Road, 1928.

To the far left, at the high desk, is Mr Harold Hughes who was in charge of advertising and exports in conjunction with John Noel Nichols. Many of the photographs and adverts featured in this book were collected and sometimes annotated by him. Bill Lee, in the centre with long shorts, joined the firm as an office junior in 1928 at the age of fourteen. His weekly wage was 12s. By the age of seventeen he had joined the team of seven sales representatives who were now covering the whole of Great Britain. He went on to become sales manager and a director of the board in 1977, retiring in 1980 after 52 years of service. Marjorie Stevenson, sitting at the low table, was secretary to John Noel Nichols until 1972.

The fleet of VIMTO vans with their drivers, 1928.

Local deliveries of VIMTO cordial in bottles, VIMTO concentrate, together with packed pills and potions and bagged herbs and spices would be made in these vans to herbalist shops, temperance bars, cafés, corner shops and bottling agents. Goods for the rest of Britain would be sent by rail, with the products for export being taken to Liverpool or Salford Docks for transportation along the Manchester Ship Canal to the sea.

The Works

'The VIMTO Department', Ayres Road, 1928. 20-gallon barrels of double-strength VIMTO ready for export to Rangoon are being prepared. Tom Broadhurst, who at the age of sixteen helped in the first mixing of VIMTO in 1908, is to the left of the picture. He had been promoted to works manager and retired in 1961.

The Packing Room, Ayres Road, 1928. VIMTO was now being sold to hundreds of mineral water manufcturers at home and in over thirty countries abroad. It was held in 10-gallon glass carboys and 6-gallon stoneware jars packed in wooden cases with wood wool. The herbs, spices, barks and roots were stored in the warehouse in rows of large wooden bins. Orders would be scooped out and weighed into paper bags ready for despatch to the herbalist.

Mixing vats of VIMTO **concentrate in the Ayres Road factory, 1928.**
The wooden vat on the left would have been double-strength, destined for Dublin, the Isle of Man, South America, Jersey and Guernsey. Relatives of the staff have fond memories of visiting the factory when they were children and being offered a big glass of VIMTO made from cordial straight from the vat. The company itself would macerate and extract flavours from the dried herbs which go to make up the unique VIMTO taste.

The Pill Packing and Labelling Room, Ayres Road, 1928.
Pills were bought in bulk, measured and scooped into small round boxes, which in turn were mounted by elastic on to card. Bottles of VIMTO cordial, which had been filled by hand with a jug and funnel, were also labelled by the team of 14-year-old girl school leavers in this room. The first mechanised bottle filling machine, consisting of a simple suction pump which filled two bottles at a time, was installed in the factory in 1938. It was not until the late 1940s that a fully mechanised process was introduced.

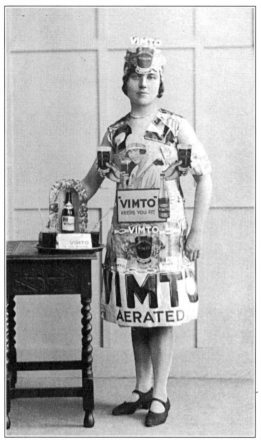

LEFT. A woman in VIMTO fancy dress, southern England, late 1920s. Her costume is adorned with showcards and labels. In the interwar period, children and adults sometimes went to fancy dress events as the representation of a branded product.

BELOW. The procession display of T. M. Barker, the bottling agent for the Pontefract district, 1927. The *papier maché* bottle shield was powered by youthful volunteers who would be offered a few bottles of VIMTO in return for walking the streets.

2

This Speciality is Advertised all over the Kingdom

IN ORDER TO BE ADVERTISED, a branded product or service needs to be of a standard and repeatable quality and in reliable supply. It should fulfil the manufacturer's promises and live up to its brand image or at least be good value for money so that it is bought more than once. New markets cannot be won and held without advertising to introduce and support the product. Noel Nichols realised this from the start and the early catalogues announced 'up-to-date showcards and advertising matter supplied. In fact we sell it for you'. A give-away diary for bottling agents and retailers of 1934 advised,

> we continue to advertise "VIMTO" throughout the British Isles, both in the press, on the screen, and by other means, and we trust that you will derive some measure of benefit from these forms of publicity. If you will co-operate with us in this respect by showing the advertising matter which we send to you from time to time we should be grateful.

The company has always advertised in a wide variety of ways: from the early showcards to 'shelf talkers'; still cinema adverts to television commercials; and large walking bottles to inflated bouncing castles. One unique taste and name has survived a diversity of personalities and descriptions but has always held the public's favour.

The showcard

The showcard used by many companies to advertise their products, throws light on the changing values, lifestyles and fashions of the people to whom they tried to appeal. Even the forms of advertising can reflect changing patterns. For example, in the mid-1960s the showcard on the counter of the corner shop disappeared and was replaced by the label promotion on the bottle on the supermarket shelf.

The showcard advertising brand names first made its appearance on the counters and walls of shops and places of refreshment in the 1880s, when mass produced, standardised and sometimes pre-packaged or bottled goods were first manufactured. Chromo-lithographic printing techniques had also reached a high standard of quality, and served a mass market. Ranging in size from a few inches up to two feet in height, they were printed or mounted onto stiff card. They could either be stood up by a cardboard prop at the back, or hung on silken cord threaded through two eyelet holes. The more elaborate showcards were 'cut-outs'. Bottle display stands, using

Exhibition Stand at City Hall, Manchester, February 1921. The company expanded rapidly after World War I when VIMTO began to be bottled under franchise to Mineral Water Manufacturers. It exhibited annually at City Hall, displaying products and promotional material which were supplied. This photograph shows showcards, blotters and decorated china casks, many of which now form part of the company's advertising collection.

ingenious cardboard engineering, presented the actual product. Designed to be colourful and eye-catching, the showcards had an illustration, the name of the product and a catchy phrase or one-line joke or statement. They made the potential customer aware that the product was available in that particular outlet, and gave a hint at what it might do for him or her. In the case of VIMTO, it would refresh you, 'Keep You Fit' or be 'The ideal Beverage for Radiant Health'.

The first images used to advertise VIMTO were not specific to the product. Showcards and blotters depicting elegant women were chosen from a batch of samples and the advertising slogan added by over-printing or simply by using pen and ink. It was the mid-1920s that saw the first humorous advertisements,

It is "VIMTO"
"VIMTO" is it.

LEFT.The engaging 'Ruth' had the original clever phrase 'It is VIMTO, VIMTO is it' positioned below her. The use of the word 'it', as in 'Try our unique speciality Vimto' was used in catalogues and promotional material long before the 'Coke is it' campaigns of the 1980s.

DRINK

SPARKLING

"VIMTO"

—o—

DELICIOUS.

PLEASE USE THIS BLOTTER.

THOROUGHBRED
"Vimto"
Not how cheap, but how good.

ABOVE. Showcard (detail) from the early 1920s. A confident and smart horsewoman declares that VIMTO is a quality 'fancy' drink, worth paying a little extra for.

ABOVE. Blotter with the illustration entitled *His Ring*, early 1920s.

Poster depicting the popular cinema and variety show star, Patricia Kirkwood, late 1940s. The pose of the model, the setting and the slick airbursh technique used by the artist Isole Armstrong evoked the popular 'Varga Girl' pin-ups created by Alfredo Vargas during World War II.

with unique subjects specific to the product and with integral captions. Until the employment of a new advertising agency in 1934, freelance designers would stroll into the office with an idea which was either commissioned or rejected. The bulk of the colour prints were chromo-lithographs giving a depth and strength of colour with a slight visual texture, enhancing the three-dimensional effect.

In 1934 the Nichols company appointed the Manchester based Osborne-Peacock Co. Ltd as its advertising agency. The original role of an agent, in the nineteenth century, had been to book advertising space in newspapers and magazines on behalf of its clients. At the beginning of the century only a handful provided any creative services, in the form of copy-writing or design. Nichols had had several agencies booking space for them, but provided the copy and commissioned the illustrations themselves. By the 1930s the agencies and the personalities who ran them started to play an increasingly important part in the public presentation of many products.

Showcard, early 1950s.

Bottle display card cut-out to sit on the neck of a bottle, early 1950s.

The Nichols company continued to deal with cinema advertisements through a special agency, as well as placing orders for the promotional novelties and the shop or café signs. However the newspaper advertising and design, and the production of showcards, was taken over by the agency, albeit with strong involvement from the company.

It was under the influence of the new agency that there appeared a spate of show-cards and calendars depicting glamorous women advertising the product. Unlike the early advertisements, which simply depicted a charming female, the mid-1930s showcards at least showed them with the drink itself, and so made the image more specific. The type of women themselves, however, could also be seen

advertising many other products from the period, such as 4711 Vanishing Cream or Aspro.

During the Second World War, due to paper and printing ink restrictions and the non-availability of branded products, showcards were not produced. The theme which emerged on showcards, bottle display cards and in the press in the late 1940s was that of VIMTO as 'A

Drink for all the Family'. The classic two-parent, two-child family, all with a distinctly American air about them, with gleaming health and full of enthusiasm for VIMTO.

Particularly notable is a set of four show-cards by the *Punch* cartoonist Herbert Stanley Terry, one published each year in the early 1950s. Diverse in subject and broad in appeal, they would have found their way to most corner shops, cafés, fish and chip shops, sporting venues and clubs. The Stan Terry series was destined to be one of the last inventive coloured graphics to be commissioned until recent times. Thereafter, the 1950s also saw a bland series of showcards, and calendars depicting women who found 'Britain's Best Beverage . . . Delicious and Exhilarating', whether going out to a dance, rowing a boat, lying at the edge of the sea or playing with their children. Many were taken from stock images and over-printed with specific text, as had been done at the beginning of the century.

Point-of-sale today

Point-of-sale advertising is important in re-awakening the half-forgotten resolution to buy, made when the potential customer has been favourably influenced by other forms of advertising. The showcard and bottle display stand had virtually disappeared by the end of the 1960s with the establishment of the supermarkets and cash and carry stores. With almost no shelf or wall space and a great variety of brand names, these outlets had no place for an individual product to be advertised. The label and packaging, and occasionally shelf signage, became the only communication with the busy shopper at the time of purchase.

'Shelf talkers' have taken on a number of forms. The thick paper 'shelf wobbler', often depicting a life-size can, was designed to dangle and attract attention. However, they proved unpopular with retail outlets as they cluttered the place and soon looked tatty. They are still occasionally used in cash and carry wholesale warehouses. No doubt they will become the collectable advertising ephemera of the future. A variety of shaped signs and banners giving information or highlighting products have been designed to be attached to shelving. Nowadays the national supermarkets prefer to use their own point-of-sale material, with limited manufacturer promotional activity, and then only at a price. It is left to the labelling and packaging of the product to declare itself to the self-service shopper.

Tailor-made fixtures and fittings

The showcard was the most consistently used and effective form of advertising issued by the company from the early days through to the 1960s. But in addition, there was a vast and imaginative range of other items, all carrying the VIMTO name, which were given away free to shops, cafés and clubs. The Advertising Ledger records the company's promotional activities from 1933 until the early 1970s. The novel fixtures and fittings which were installed in numerous outlets included enamelled door finger plates, clocks, billiard room shades and elaborate mirrored signs and shelves. VIMTO bottle labels were adapted as menu holders or else special menus bearing the VIMTO name were printed. Simple glasses with the words 'ALWAYS DRINK VIMTO' were supplied from the 1920s through to the 1950s. These appear regularly in the showcards of the period with the characters depicted holding them up, catching your eye and almost joining you for a drink. Unfortunately, as yet, there are none of the glasses, nor any of the other bespoke fittings in the VIMTO Advertising Collection.

The china kegs and hot water urns of the 1920s and '30s, emblazoned with the VIMTO name, could be bought, but a wide variety of VIMTO dispensers was rented out to cafés from 1954 through to the early '70s. The 1950s also saw the arrival of the flat yellow metal ashtray, which was made without a cigarette rest so as to avoid the purchase tax on ashtrays. It doubled up as a coaster and was delivered in bulk with the showcards to the cafés and fish and chip shops.

Outdoor signs

A significant part of the creation of VIMTO awareness, to use a modern advertising phrase, was the use of signs on the exteriors of the cafés and shops which sold VIMTO. The first enamelled iron signs, put up in 1936, were a combination of red, black and white and declared simply 'Drink "VIMTO"' and 'Most Refreshing' or 'The Tonic Fruit Drink'. There were also smaller signs angled out from the wall. The traveller, or salesman, would encourage the shop or café owner to provide a rent-free space for quality enamelled signs, which came in a variety of shapes and sizes. The list of orders would be sent to the manufacturers, Burnham and Company, in London, and they would gradually install them. When the signs were fixed, a voucher would be completed to show that the work had been done. On his next visit, no doubt the traveller would inspect the work. He was also responsible for cleaning the signs with wire wool each time he visited to take the orders and deliver the showcards and novelties. This procedure continued well into the early 1960s, but thereafter they all disappeared. A few found their way back to the VIMTO factory while others are in museums, or on the walls of nostalgia restaurants, or in the hands of collectors.

Because of the shortage and expense of steel after the war, other materials were used for signage carrying the VIMTO name. Both perspex and aluminium were used for a few signs. The first red fired glass bands or pelmets, which were fixed to window fronts with a fine cement, appeared in 1948. They came in two heights and were made by Soffe Bros. of Urmston, who charged for them by the foot. A combination of phrases could emblazon a window. Together with the usual 'DRINK "VIMTO" Most Refreshing', the words 'SNACK BAR', 'FISH AND CHIPS', 'SWEETS', or 'ICES' could be chosen by the café owner. These glass bands were easily broken by bicycles being propped up against them and became too expensive to replace. However, plans are being made to substitute them with plastic window stickers. These less permanent signs allow for changing advertising themes as well as catching the customer's eye with each new design.

Mrs Tarbrook's Temperance Bar, Malin Bridge, Sheffield, 1959.
Many of the individual advertisements for VIMTO were instigated by café owners or bottling agents.
Posters, canvas window blinds, delivery vans, mirrors and painted walls all sported the VIMTO name
alongside that of the owners. This post-war example was first painted in 1949 at the company's
expense after they had approved the design.

The first recorded electric sign was a one off 'Opaline Geode' advertising VIMTO costing £1 10s. for Mr James Haslam's establishment in Blackpool; one wonders what it looked like. But it was the late 1930s before Burnham Signs produced double-sided electronic box advertisements, with a separate panel for the trade name. Sometimes the local council refused permission for the signs to be installed, and many were taken down during the Second World War. A few expensive neon signs appeared in 1939 at £12 each;

these required maintenance by an electrician every three months.

Individual advertisements

The advertising ledger also briefly describes hundreds of one-off ideas from the 1930s, for promoting the product. These were usually produced at the instigation of the café or shop owner, or of the bottling agent. Individual posters, advertisements framed in glass, canvas window blinds and painted walls, all sported the VIMTO name, together with that of the owner.

A more conventional mobile advertisement appeared on delivery vans. Apart from being on the fleet of red delivery trucks owned by the company, the VIMTO name appeared on delivery trucks throughout the British Isles and abroad. When a new vehicle was bought, or an old one repainted, the mineral water company would share the painting costs with J. N. Nichols and Company. Trucks were also temporarily decorated with showcards as floats for local carnivals or processions. John Esperner and Son of Loftus wrote a letter in 1926 saying 'We decorated our Rolley with your VIMTO showcards and distributed VIMTO free as an advert' at the annual carnival in the town.

Advertisements for VIMTO on tramcars and buses in the Manchester and Liverpool areas, in the Midlands and on the Isle of Man appeared sporadically until the late 1940s. They took the form of a transparency lit from behind on the inside, or else a painted sign attached to the upper or lower deck of the vehicle, usually saying 'DRINK VIMTO'. In 1987,

a 1930s' tramcar which had been sponsored by the company and was bedecked with advertisements for the drink, trundled up and down the Promenade at Blackpool as a reminder of times gone by.

Promotional novelties

Fortunately, samples of many of the free gifts given away by retailers and café owners to their VIMTO customers have been saved by the company. These included novelty postcards, football fixtures, bus timetables, blotters, packets of pins, bottle openers and card games. Another form of printed matter spreading the VIMTO name was the free provision of batches of 10,000 'Whist Cards for Café Drives' for the large cinemas in the 1930s. The most treasured and well known of the VIMTO novelties is the little *Vimto Book of Knowledge*, to use its most recent title, which was first published during the First World War. In the past, the books were given away in bulk to bottling agents to distribute to their customers. Schools would also write directly asking for copies. Children were informed of the intention that every child in Britain should receive a copy. It was hoped that children would educate themselves to a better life in terms of knowledge, speech and behaviour. There were two editions during World War I—the first was known as *The Little Blue Book for Scholars* and the second, with a red cover, was entitled *The Little VIMTO Book for Scholars*. The next edition in the company's collection, dating from the late 1920s, is *The New VIMTO Book for Scholars*, with a rose cover depicting a schoolboy and

ABOVE: Six editions of the 'VIMTO Book'. This treasured little book was very much in keeping with Noel Nichols' personal creed of 'self-instruction'.

RIGHT: Illustration from *The New* VIMTO *Book for Scholars*, 1949.

girl. From then on, the books are conveniently dated on the page carrying the explanation of roman numerals. 'Famous Discoveries and Inventions' are updated each time, but the 'Notes on Etiquette' and the 'Farthing Table' disappeared long ago. In more recent times, the book has been sent out free, directly to the customer, in return for a set number of labels or ring-pull tabs. Future editions should prove even more popular, as a result of the recent popularity of quiz nights, slot machines and TV quiz shows, all of which test people's general knowledge.

On-pack offers

Today, gifts and novelties are posted to the customer direct, in return for proof of purchase of Nichols' products. Sometimes they are free, with the addition of post and packing costs, or a nominal charge is made in the case of the larger promotions. Their initial purpose is to entice lapsed or uninitiated drinkers into buying the product. Once VIMTO is tasted, subsequent purchases are more likely. Label promotions also act as a 'thank you' to loyal VIMTO drinkers. Special labels are printed, with a flash on the front one to draw attention to the offer detailed on the back label. Bottle neck collars are also used. Cash and carry wholesalers, supermarket chains and retailers are encouraged to stock the drink as it is perceived as giving extra value to the customer. Label promotions are featured in the editorial comment of the trade press which is sometimes the only direct form of communication between the manufacturer and buyer. Individually tailored promotion packages are also arranged with leading supermarket chains. Recent promotions sporting the VIMTO name have included models of a 1934 bus and a 1927 lorry, T-shirts, a set of postcards reproducing the old showcards, 'bum bags', ceramic name plates, china mugs, and cameras.

A comic called *The Vimto*, featuring 'Max the Bulldog' and 'Fizzy Lizzie' was published as an offer in 1988 and included many bespoke items such as roll-up wallets, aprons and keyring torches sold at special prices. The bulldog was enlisted to help with sales because it is seen as synonymous with the British. VIMTO was being promoted again as 'The Great British Drink' in reaction to the infiltration and dominance of American brands. A real dog with a long pedigree by the name of 'Merriveen McClean of Bullzaye', known to his friends as 'Dougie' was chosen to appear at trade fairs and to open supermarkets. He was featured prominently on cans of VIMTO until 1989, when market research discovered that he gave the sparkling drink a childish image, unacceptable to the teenage market; Max was abandoned shortly afterwards.

Exhibition souvenirs

Souvenirs from the travelling exhibition upon which this book is based have incorporated the old advertising images. The strength of colour and bold design of the early showcards translate well onto key rings, tea towels and a jigsaw, the latter being a montage of the collection. Tin Box International Ltd., London, have added to their range nine new

'Max', the bulldog, promoted VIMTO in the 1980s.

storage tins which use the early advertising to good effect. Garnier and Co. Ltd., also of London, have produced a set of four high quality enamelled signs featuring the Stan Terry showcards. Postcards published by Santoro Graphics, of Rotherham, have also been popular.

Company publications

Until the Second World War catalogues played an essential part in the home and export trade. The first catalogue of goods for sale was a simple two-sided leaflet. Illustrations appeared in the much enlarged catalogue of the early 1920s, which also had a full colour front cover picture of a cascading platter of fruit. The catalogues of the 1930s had colour illustrations of the bottled products on the inside, as well as sample labels. The exquisite gouache artwork for these bottle illustrations is still in the collection.

Nowadays glossy coloured leaflets and *Nichols News* give information on new products, changing forms of packaging, advertising campaigns and sponsorships. They are sprinkled liberally with current public relations and marketing phrases such as 'year-on-year growth', 'massive TV spend' and 'brand backing'. Designed and originated using computer graphics, there is no longer any tangible artwork to collect. The corporate video is also employed to present the products and highlight the success of the company.

The printed page

VIMTO was advertised in newspapers and trade publications prior to 1915. Until 1933, the copy was written by Noel Nichols and the export manager, Mr Hughes. The designs for illustrated advertisements, typesetting and printing blocks were commissioned directly from a pool of artists. Advertising agents such as the Expert Advertising Company would undertake the administrative side, placing advertisements in the national and local press, and charging a percentage commission.

In the 1920s there were plenty of popular newspapers and magazines giving lively reports of the news. Together with club journals, cinema, and sporting programmes, advertising on the printed page was an effective way of informing a mass market before the advent of commercial radio in 1932 and television in 1955. A particular section of the community could be targeted through the publications it read. The advertisements told the reader what the drink was like, what it could do for him or her, and how much it cost. They also said where VIMTO was available: 'Sold wherever Mineral Waters are obtainable'.

Preserved in a press cuttings file is a set of light-hearted, tongue-in-cheek illustrated advertisements dating from 1928 to 1934. As it is in advertising today, they rarely gave any hint of the poverty and harshness which existed in the wider world—in this case the Great Depression of 1929–33. They just tried to encourage people to smile a little. The language used is cheery and frightfully proper. A story was told, in the way that television commercials tell a tale today, and the 'before and after' theme was used imaginatively. The advertisements also reflect the interests and lifestyles of the readers of the time.

Occasional advertisements appeared in children's publications. Boy Scout Association handbooks advised Scouts to 'Be prepared' when buying mineral water. 'Don't ask for a drink, and leave it to the shopkeeper to give you any sort. Say "VIMTO".' The youth of Britain were encouraged to exercise their consumer choice. The VIMTO essay competition appeared in *The Guide*, *Adventurer*, *Hotspur*, *Rover*, *Wizard* and *The Skipper* in March 1937. The subject was 'Why I Like "VIMTO"', and required a bottle label to be sent in with the entry. The cash prize winners' names and addresses were later published.

VIMTO was also advertised in a great diversity of other publications, ranging from the *Stretford Conservative Year Book* to the *Manchester Working Men's Club and Institute Periodical*. Both the Catholic and Protestant Whit Walk programmes held VIMTO advertisements. Even the *Salford Masonic Hall Ladies Bazaar*

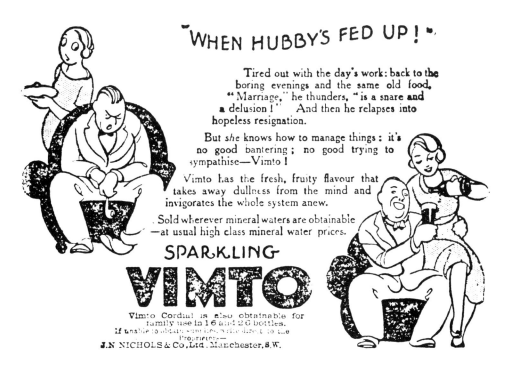

Newspaper advertisement, 1929.

Bazaar Committee Recipe and Quotation Book had a half-page advertisement in 1935. The student population was also informed of the wonders of VIMTO in the handbooks and 'rag mags' of Manchester University and The Royal Technical College at Peel Park, Salford. One advertisement in Manchester City Football Club's programme, *Blue and White,* of December 1929, declared 'SPEED . . . that is the trend of modern life. Faster and faster—unless we take precautions health will suffer'. VIMTO offered aid so that one could 'live the strenuous life without the strain'. The same advertisement would be even more meaningful today.

In 1934 the Osborne–Peacock agency of Manchester had been appointed to arrange for the advertising in the press all over Brit-

ain. The advertising ledger records the exact publications and costs involved. Surprisingly, VIMTO was advertised regularly throughout the years of the Second World War, even though the product could not be bought. This was acknowledged in the copy—'Just to remind you of "VIMTO" ' and 'Something to look forward to when the Victory is won'. One advertisement in 1942 referred topically to ' "VIMTO" and the Beverage Plan'. In that year, Sir William Beveridge had published his highly influential and well-publicised *Report on Social Insurance and Allied Services* which set out the basic principles upon which the post-war Welfare State was to be based.

Advertising in the trade press has been a consistent activity of the company. Until the Second World War, bottling companies were encouraged to become sole agents for carbonated VIMTO in their area. In the 1950s and beyond, the emphasis was changed to attract business from the retailers, large and small. As in the 1930s, VIMTO cordial was pushed as a winter drink which always sold well.

Advertising to the general public in the national newspapers continued until the early 1960s, but with the increasing effectiveness of commercial television as a mass medium, they were phased out. However, of late, competitions such as 'Spot the difference' illustrations with worthwhile prizes have appeared in many local papers nationwide. Women's glossy magazine advertisements, in conjunction with television campaigns or posters in bus shelters, are now part of the annual advertising strategy, though they are regarded as secondary to television as a medium.

Vimto on the screen

The company has kept up with most new advertising trends. At least as early as 1928, VIMTO adverts on glass slides were projected on to cinema screens in the north west of England and India. Some were photographs of showcards alongside additional text, while others were taken from commissioned artwork. It was also in 1928 that the first talkies were heard in the picture houses, and Noel Nichols soon had personal shares in British Talking Pictures Ltd.

Although television had been invented in 1925, the first transmissions of commercial television did not begin until 1955 through a network of contractors supervised by the Independent Television Authority. It provided

a new and exciting challenge to manufacturers and their advertising agents to present their product to the growing audience of television viewers. The Nichols company soon commissioned its first advertisement for this new form of promotion.

Despite the new medium, the themes for advertising VIMTO were much the same as those used in the pre-war period—thirst-quenching or warming; good value; and drunk by all. The advertising of any health-giving properties of the drink had been dropped following a series of Food Description Acts which were introduced with the new National Health Service. Only patent medicines could claim any advantage to health. Despite being first registered with a medicines trademark, VIMTO was now firmly presented and perceived as a soft drink. The cordial label described it as 'Delicious' and 'Non-alcoholic'.

The Nichols Company made its first commercial in 1956, with the Osborne-Peacock agency. Brief details in the Advertising Ledger tell us only that it cost £112 16s. to make, which included £2 10s. for two VIMTO story boards, £90 production costs, and fees of £20 6s. paid to '2 children and 1 man'. This would have been a simple, very economical black and white commercial, projected from 35mm film on to a screen for the television cameras to film. A straightforward commercial today can cost from £100,000 to produce. In 1956 a fifteen-second showing on 'Evening Time' Granada Television cost £120, while the 'Run of the day' spots cost only £30. Today a similar spot in the evening would cost £8,000.

WET your WHISTLE with VIMTO

MRS HOWARTH, BROOKS' ICES.

14, RAILWAY ST., Ramsbottom

Cinema advertisement, 1930s.

The first full-colour television commercial was made in the mid-1970s, once the benchmark whereby 50 per cent of household sets were in colour had been reached. This fun advertisement, entitled 'There are Plenty Different Ways to Drink your VIMTO', set out to show how versatile the drink was in both its sparkling and cordial forms. It shook off the staid image vimto had acquired, with the use of pop music and zany actions. Today television takes up the bulk of the advertising budget. New commercials are used to give consumers information on changes in product and packaging. The two different markets—for the cordial and canned carbonate forms of VIMTO—confirmed by market research, are now targeted with their own commercials shown around appropriate television programmes. The humorous and light-hearted nature of the showcards is, however, still maintained.

Public relations

When the Nichols company was floated on the stock market in 1961 a public relations

Photographs taken in a banana plantation in Jamaica, 1968, during the filming of a commercial for Sparkling VIMTO which was shown on British television. The children arrived by horse-drawn cart at the beach and in true pirate fashion dug up a treasure chest full of bottles and cans of the precious ruby nectar. The slides, taken by the father of two of the children who lived at a nearby village, recently came to light and are the only record.

company was appointed to issue press releases concerning the financial results at each half-year and year-end. In the early 1980s Prosper Communications had the task of increasing VIMTO's profile, either by finding and developing stories, or by creating events which would appeal to the media and the public. JGPR of Manchester have been the public relations company since 1986. Press releases and photographs covering all the company's activities are regularly sent out and well received. The publicity photographs in the archive have a distinctive style. As they will be seen only once amidst many other photographs and news stories they are usually posed and obvious in subject. Judith Patten PR have been successfully promoting the travelling exhibition and this book since 1994.

A press cuttings agency supplies a record of VIMTO's appearances in the media. The name VIMTO pops up all over the place in magazines and newspapers. When making a suggested list of ten artists for the National Gallery's Sainsbury Wing, one journalist for *You* magazine suggested 'Leonardo da VIMTO'. A horse named 'VIMTO' was featured when he was saved by the Horses and Ponies Protection Association. When discussing new trade deals with the Russian Federation, a writer in *The Independent* mused on 'mountains of Eccles Cakes and lakes of VIMTO' forming. When the shares in J. N. Nichols (VIMTO) plc are tipped or the financial results

The VIMTO Bouncy Castle was used for the sponsored bounces which raised funds for county cricket clubs in 1992. Chris Sefton, Group Marketing Manager, tested the 'bounce factor' with Somerset County professionals.

covered, phrases such as 'sparkling perform-ance' or 'profits fizzed up' often appear. The drink has also been described variously as 'that ruby coloured nectar', a 'dark elixir' and an 'eponymous fizzy drink'.

VIMTO is also mentioned in television shows. Jasper Carrott, Griff Rhys-Jones and Mel Smith, along with Victoria Wood, have all made reference to it in their comedy sketches. It has also been used by Diedre's daughter in *Coronation Street*, and a bottle of vimto has been men-tioned rather less salubriously by Rik Mayall in *Bottom*. *Red Dwarf* and *Spitting Image* similarly discuss the drink. VIMTO was de-scribed as a 'cultural icon' by Robert Ro-binson when the drink was featured on *Pick of the Week*. It also often appears in disguise as stage red wine or port in the theatre and on television.

A posed publicity photograph of Olympic silver medallist, Shirley Strong, triumphant over John Nichols after the fitness challenge, Wythenshawe factory, 1986. Members of the Nichols family and staff appear in the background.

In 1988 the company sponsored Rick Astley's first UK concert tour. In conjunction, a promotion competition for tickets was held on cans..

Brand awareness through sponsorship

Today companies can make statements about themselves and their products by association with the individuals or schemes which they sponsor. At the events themselves and through media coverage, the name can appear in many different contexts. Sponsorship is also a way of supporting worthwhile undertakings in the society which supports a company's existence. Individual sportspeople and groups have received the benefit of Nichols sponsorship. In 1984 Nick Sanders was sponsored to undertake gruelling cycle tours to the source of the River Nile and around Britain's coast—naturally taking a supply of VIMTO to sustain him. Shirley Strong, the hurdler and Olympic silver medallist, training for the Commonwealth Games team in 1986, was offered sponsorship on one condition—she had to beat John Nichols in a fitness test involving sit-ups, press-ups and squat thrusts. Predictably, she was successful and newspaper and television companies gave enthusiastic coverage. At a more general level, the main charitable sponsorship from 1988 for four years was the Duke of Edinburgh

Award, aimed at providing a broadly based programme of activities for all fourteen- to twenty-five-year-olds. The scheme to encourage young people to participate was promoted on bottle labels. County cricket has received long-term support from the Nichols company.

In the early 1980s the self-appointed 'Nottingham University VIMTO Appreciation Society' (NUVAS) imbibed vast quantities of VIMTO while its members were studying to be doctors and lawyers. The company has had its own VIMTO Drinkers' Club for which a certificate of membership was issued.

The Vimto Worldbeaters

Under the guidance of the public relations company, a number of challenges to existing world records, as recorded in the *Guinness Book of Records* have been attempted and achieved. A pyramid of empty VIMTO cans (1989), a hand-painted jigsaw (1991), and a champagne glass fountain overflowing with VIMTO (1992) have all been well publicised. They have been undertaken as projects for local polytechnics. The most recent and ambitious attempt was to break the record for the world's biggest working yo-yo (1993).

As unique in taste as it was when it was first made in 1908, VIMTO has been promoted in a myriad different ways over the years. Its image has been a reflection of the lifestyles or aspirations of its drinkers. The Nichols company has always tried to fulfil the needs of the day in an interesting way, with the phrases and images used to describe VIMTO being responsive to their times.

Novelties

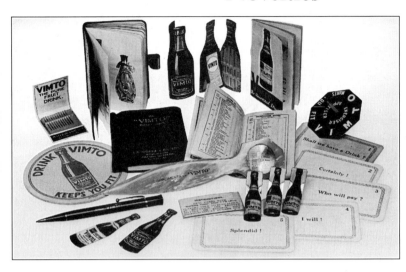

Selection of VIMTO novelties from the 1920s. This includes an imitation matchbook containing pins, a magnifying glass, a handy set of needles and pins, clickers, football fixtures and a card game for deciding who should buy the next round of hot VIMTOS. The metal spinner is flat and indented with the word 'YOU' at the end. This was spun until it stopped and pointed at at someone.

Novelty postcard, mid-1920s.
As the 'turn up slowly' tab is lifted, the bottle of VIMTO is guzzled by the schoolboy.

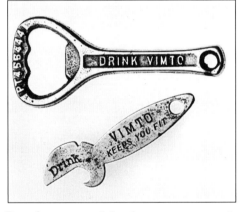

Bespoke crown cork bottle openers, 1937 and early 1930s.
A handy patented bottle opener described in its specification of 1937 as an 'improved manually operated prising tool for removing metal closure caps from bottles' was much sought after. Apart from being an obvious soft drink give-away, it was new in that it deformed the crown cork which 'can well obviate fraudulent use of the once-used cap'. It continued to be produced well into the 1950s.

Cinema advert, late 1920s.

Painted lead novelty, late 1920s.
This dapper gentleman with trilby, walking stick and spats, propping up the bar with a glass of VIMTO to hand, was also seen in a newspaper and cinema advert of the same period. With his sharp features and smart attire, he looked a little like Noel Nichols.

'The VIMTO Collection' on-pack offers, 1993.
Gifts and good value novelties appealing to children and teenagers now have to be sent away for. The label rather than the local grocer becomes the main line of communication between manufacturer and consumer. As in the past, the items such as digital watches and bum-bum bags reflect the era from which they come.

The "Vimto" Times.

"Some People won't believe there is a Silver Lining to every cloud until aeroplanes are so cheap that they can go and see for themselves."

| Manchester. | Not registered as a Newspaper. | May, 1926. | Price :- Free. |

"VIMTO" PARS.

1 Our entrance to this world is naked and bare
Our journey through life is trouble and care
Our egress from here we know not where
But if we do well here, we do well there.

2 The man who means the most, does the most and says the least.

3 The wear and tear of rust is greater than the wear and tear of work.

Try "VIMTO"

It refreshes at once.

STRIKE LIMERICK.

We print below a Limerick and offer a Prize of £2 2s. 0d. to the sender of what is considered to be the best line to complete it.

Replies to be sent in to THE NAP NOVELTY CO. 32/34 KENNEDY STREET, MANCHESTER, not later than Friday, May 21st.

A Lady just told us she'd like us,
To offer advice to the strikers,
She said : "Now VIMTO,
If you give it to Joe - -

All efforts submitted will receive careful consideration, but the Editors decision shall be final, and no correspondence regarding the competition can be entertained.

IT'S GOOD   WHAT'S GOOD ?

WHY "VIMTO" OF COURSE

EDITOR'S CHAT.

CARRY ON, ALL'S WELL.

The "VIMTO" TIMES is issued at this period by the proprietors of "VIMTO" with the supreme hope that, if only for a brief moment, it will divert the attention of it's readers from any too serious anxiety or unnecessary worry.

"VIMTO" itself, as an energising, rejuvanating tonic drink, made from the finest herbs and fruits, has a simply marvellous effect in making one look on the bright side of things.

It is worth all the money in the world to be able to cultivate a cheery outlook on life.

GET THE "VIMTO" HABIT, a glass a day drives dull care away.

Millions drink it and acclaim it. Go thou and do likewise !!

JOKES.

Laugh and the World laughs with you, snore and you sleep alone.

A Special Constable in Hull having occasion to pull up the driver of a vehicle owing to the name on the side being difficult to distinguish called out "The name on your waggon's obliterated."   The driver of the waggon replied "You're a liar, it's O'Brien'

A dear old lady was awaiting a train at Derby during the first days of the strike and hearing that trains were very uncertain wished to make sure of hers, so much so that she asked one of the volunteer porters three times "Does this train go to St. Pancras?"

Eventually he found the lady a seat, again she asked was she right for St. Pancras, and finding she was, called the man back, "But I've left my tin chest on the platform" The porter locked the door and replied, "I don't care if you've left your india-rubber stomach, you're stopping in that train."

Tears stood in the eyes of Bernard Cohen, his hand shook and dire trouble marked his usually placid and innocent brow. "Everthing vos against me" he wailed, "vhy haf I deserved it ?" Vot's the matter asked his friend Elvy Lewis. "Vell I tell you, I haf just taken a peautiful varehouse and filled it mit my finest goods, den as a matter of brecaution I insure it all and now der landlord has let der second floor to an agent for Fire Extinguishers for a showroom and now to-day if he ain't gone and let der ground floor for to make a swimming bath."

STRIKE DONT'S.

DON'T lose your nerve, "VIMTO" will help you to keep it or restore it.

DON'T repeat idle rumours.

DON'T lose your temper however trying the situation. Drink "VIMTO" and KEEP COOL.

DON'T hoard food. a glass of "VIMTO" will sustain you.

DON'T look glum, KEEP SMILING, remember Jonah and the Whale, he came out alright.

DON'T forget "VIMTO" in your enforced walks to town, it will make you forget your strike and make miles appear as yards.

DON'T forget when your coal runs out that "VIMTO" will keep you cheerful.

Get "VIM-TO" win through.

NEWS.

There appears to be no shortage of petrol and there appears to be no truth in the rumour that it is to be rationed, we would request our readers not to use cars for pleasure during the strike, "VIMTO" is not a luxury but a necessity. Drink "VIMTO" and KEEP FIT.

STOP PRESS NEWS.

Later news, if any will be published in this column or we will "GIVE IT TO JOE."

Latest about the mines :- Mine's a "VIMTO" How to keep warm with one sack of coal for a month. Run up and down the stairs with the coal on your back.

SMILE D - - - YOU, SMILE.

Are We Downhearted ? NO-o-o-o

"VIMTO"

THE TONIC FRUIT DRINK.

The *"Vimto" Times* published during the days of The Great Strike, May 1926.

Printed on one side of a single page, The *"Vimto" Times* imitated the news-sheets which were published by both the government and unions instead of newspapers which were produced only intermittently during the nine days of the strike. The VIMTO company was not unionised and business continued as best it could. The delivery vans containing both supplies for herbalists as well as VIMTO itself carried posters indicating that only food and medicines were being carried, enabling them to get through the picket lines. John Noel Nichols gave hitch-hikers a lift to work in exchange for a donation in a box for Dr Barnardo's.

'Life Is Sweeter with VIMTO'

Newspaper advert, 1929.
Before the advent of television as a visual advertising medium, humorous and knowingly corny adverts in newspapers reached a wide and varied audience.

Newspaper advert, 1929.

Newspaper advert, 1932.

For the Whole Family

Newspaper advert, 1929.

Newspaper advert, 1932.

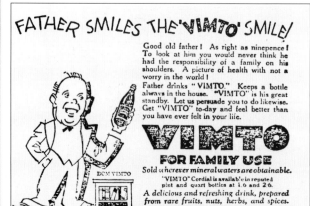

Newspaper advert, 1928.

Newspaper advert, 1932.

Newspaper adverts, 1929.
VIMTO was promoted as a special treat for all the family, especially at Christmas.

Advertising to the Trade

Trade advert, 1929.
Advertising in the trade press has been a consistent activity of the company. Until the Second World War, bottling companies were encouraged to become sole agents for carbonated VIMTO in their area. In the 1950s and beyond, the emphasis was changed to attract business from the retailers, both large and small.

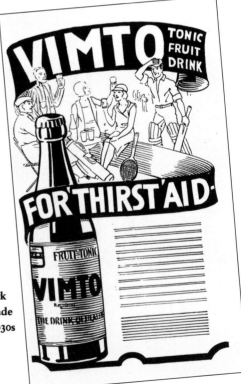

Rejected artwork for proposed trade adverts, early 1930s (pen and ink). The quips were considered just too corny!

Trade advert, July 1954.

A series of surreal adverts directed at retailers incorporated the VIMTO bottle into a variety of bizarre situations, including forming the body of a twin boom jet.

'VIMTO sales are growing higher than ever!', trade advert, 1955 (detail).

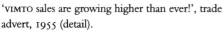

'Hot Favourite for Winter. VIMTO Cordial Served Hot or Cold! … ', trade advert, 1955 (detail).

The Art of the Showcard

***A Glamorous Woman Holding a Glass of Vimto* by Wilton Williams, late 1930s (watercolour and pastel).**

A luscious lady seductively beckons in a backless, black lace evening dress, bedecked with VIMTO-coloured roses. Wilton Williams had depicted society people in fashionable British and American illustrated magazines, and was commissioned by the Nichols company on several occasions. The original artwork for three of his showcards recently turned up again, stored behind a cupboard at the Wythenshawe office. The corresponding showcards are in the VIMTO Advertising Collection.

Showcard, late 1930s.

LEFT. *Woman in a Halter Neck Dress* by Wilton Williams, late 1930s (watercolour).

***Woman in a* VIMTO *coloured dress,* (re-touched colour photograph) 1953.**
The company was keen to be up-to-date, and the modern look was photography. The first use of a colour photograph appears on a calendar in 1954. Mr Nichols and his sons, Peter and John, were presented with a choice of heavily re-touched photographs of women with a bottle and a glass of sparkling VIMTO on a tray. The smoking lady in a fashionable VIMTO-coloured haltar neck dress was chosen and the photographic print has been kept in the company archives. Until the risks to health were fully realised, smoking was still seen as a sophisticated habit.

Showcard by Stan Terry, early 1950s. The cartoonist Herbert Stanley Terry brought his humour to a set of four showcards published in the early 1950s.

Sketch for a showcard by Stan Terry which was rejected, early 1950s, pencil. The image of a hiker on the river bank—with or without his girlfriend—was decided against, in favour of a tramp stealing a bottle of VIMTO from a fishing boy scout.

Another idea for a showcard by Stan Terry which was not chosen, early 1950s (pencil).

Dynamic Graphics

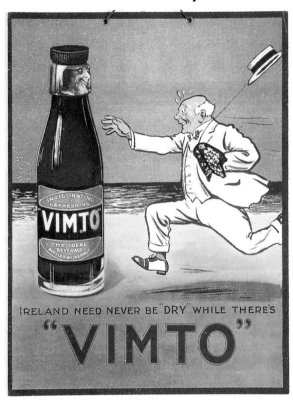

IRELAND NEED NEVER BE "DRY" WHILE THERE'S "VIMTO"

Cinema advert, late 1920s.

Showcard, mid-1920s.

The mid-1920s saw the commissioning of clever showcards and promotional novelties specific to the company's main product. The pun on the word 'dry' can be read variously to mean that the straw-boatered gentleman is thirsty; the weather is dry and hot; or that the licensing laws were restrictive. The movement of the character rushing in from the side-line and the cheerful face on the bottle would have appealed to all ages.

Bottle display card, late 1920s.

VIMTO! KEEPS YOU FIT!

Agents
T. & R. SMITH, WATER ST.
CHORLEY   TEL. 142

DRINK "VIMTO" IT KEEPS YOU FIT

BEND THIS PORTION BACK TO STAND OR PLACE ON BOTTLE NECK.

VIMTO KEEPS THE BALL ROLLING

TOE THE LINE WITH VIM
DRINK VIMTO

Showcard, mid-1920s. This particularly inventive advert by 'CHAP' simply depicts a running footballer whose body is made up with the letters of V I M T O. In contrast to the first showcards, the name of the product has become entirely integral with the illustration.

'Keeps You Fit'

Showcard, early 1930s.
The young and glamorous were depicted as keeping healthy with a glass of VIMTO every day.

Showcard, mid-1920s.
VIMTO cordial was also given a healthy image with exaggerated references to the fruit content of the drink.

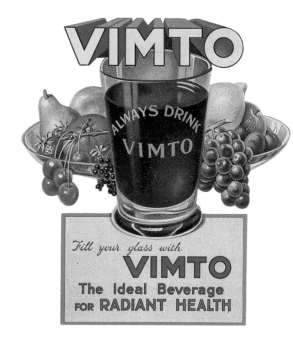

Showcard, mid-1930s.
VIMTO was promoted as a drink to keep you fit and give you energy, whatever your sport.

Showcard by Stan Terry, early 1950s. Post World War Two labelling and advertising restrictions meant phrases such as 'Keeps You Fit' and the 'Drink of Health' could no longer be used. Associations with sport were maintained, but in a satirical, humourous vein.

Changing Images of Women

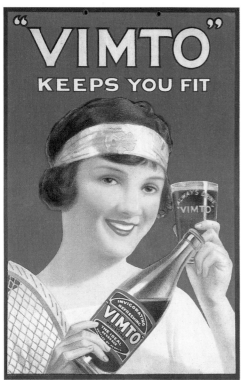

Showcard, mid-1930s.
The thirsty tennis player arriving with her friends at a temperance bar would have found herself reflected in the showcard of a fresh faced natural girl, with tousled hair, looking forward to a glass of VIMTO.

Showcard, early 1930s.
In contrast, aspirational advertising for VIMTO presented it as a quality, sophisticated beverage to be sipped by fashionable ladies who styled themselves upon Hollywood movie stars and frequented smart cafés alone.

Showcard, 1956.

The use of posed, grinning women to promote a wide variety of products now appears outmoded and facile. This showcard features an Ernest Race enamelled steel rod 'Antelope' chair and table used at the 1951 Festival of Britain. The chair came to epitomise the 'contemporary' style of British post-war furniture.

Still from the 'Roly Polys' commercial, by Tom Reddy Advertising, 1987.
Appealing initially to women, who 'need to watch their waist', the new diet version of sparkling VIMTO was perversely launched by the well-rounded, jolly Roly Polys. Little Mo declared—'Think you've got problems? Look at me!'

Actor from a scene in the 'Ain't that a Shame' carbonate commercial, Tom Reddy Advertising, 1993.
The young woman agressively challenges the potential VIMTO drinker to change their habits and try something different.

For Young and Old

Showcard for hot VIMTO cordial, mid-1930s.

In pre-World War Two newspaper adverts, parents were encouraged to give their children VIMTO at home. Oral history and written memories reveal that young customers frequented the safety of the herbalist shop and the temperance bar alone and bottles of fizzy VIMTO were a regular purchase from the corner shop. The 'VIMTO Book' given to children encouraged learning as well as the drinking of VIMTO. However, this showcard is unusual as point-of-sale material rarely appealed to children directly, despite their consumer status.

Magazine advert, 1990.

One specific campaign for VIMTO cordial for glossy women's magazines and outdoor poster sites was 'The Taste of Home' series. It was created for the Autumn and Winter of 1990 and 1991, and addressed mothers of young children whose offspring were not usually too far away from home. The Winter scene of a boy fishing with his dog, keeping warm with a hot VIMTO provided by 'Mum', was intended to create nostalgic memories for the future. The oil painting was commissioned from Keith Ritchens by Tom Reddy Advertising, with a specific brief as to subject, content and style. A limited edition of half a million 1.5 litre cordial labels featured the painting and was described as a 'collector's label'.

Showcard depicting the broad appeal of VIMTO, **by Stan Terry, early 1950s.** By the 1950s, VIMTO was a long-established drink which had appeal across three generations of people who had known it for most of their lives. The modern suburban detached house, complete with garage, garden and newly installed television aerial reflected the aspirations of many in post-war Britain.

VIMTO Appeals to All Classes

Showcard, early 1930s.
Certainly up until the Second World War, company literature declared that 'VIMTO appeals to all classes of the community, both young and old'. A showcard of a working man, complete with cloth cap and overall, declares 'I drink VIMTO, too' (as opposed to beer).

Showcard, 1933.
A lady rests on the wall of her extensive English country garden to refresh herself with a bottle of sparkling VIMTO. This image also appeared on the calendar for 1933.

Newspaper advert, 1929.
'A Desperate Man' is mollified with VIMTO by his middle-class victim, who decides to 'be matey-like'.

Artwork for a glass slide advert for the cinema by 'BALL', late 1920s (gouache).
VIMTO also made an appearance in upper-class club bars.

The New Advertising Medium

Stills of the three simple black and white scenes of the 'Hiker filmlet' shown on all but southern television stations in 1958 and 1959.

With the advent of commercial television in 1955, adverts for sparkling VIMTO soon appeared in the new medium on Granada in 1956. Television cameras filmed the images projected from 35mm film. There is no visual record of the earliest ones, but luckily 'Hiker' and 'VIMTO Family', commissioned by Osborne-Peacock, Manchester, have been saved.

**Stills of the scenes from a more
elaborate television commercial
for VIMTO cordial entitled
'VIMTO Family', 1962.**
The thirst-quenching qualities of
VIMTO cordial as a drink for all the
family continued to be promoted.

Television Commercials in the 1980s

DEREK GRIFFITHS, "One of these days you're going to check what you're drinking and try a Vimto.

Is it a Cola? Oh no. Is it just a fruit drink? No ... It's a secret.

And our Cordial gives you twenty two drinks to discover it ... but by then it's too late,

cause we've got'cha.
JINGLE
We got'cha, Vimto's gonna get'cha in the end.

"So check what you're drinking".

JINGLE
Cause Vimto's gonna get'cha in the end.

Promotional trade leaflet illustrating the Derek Griffiths television commercial for VIMTO, by Royds, Manchester, 1982 (detail).
The popular children's entertainer Derek Griffiths anticipated a brand loyalty with the theme 'We're gonna getcha in the end.' This pre-campaign leaflet warned retailers that they should stock up on VIMTO as consumer demand in response to the commercial would be great. They were right—sales of VIMTO more than doubled.

Scene from the storyboard for the proposed 'VIMTO Café' commercial, 1984.

Still from the 'VIMTO Café' commercial by Royds, Manchester, 1984.
The 'VIMTO Café' adverts, which featured many of the showcards and advertising signs from the company archives, were well received. 'Whoop it up with VIMTO' was the theme. It stressed the uniqueness of VIMTO and the exciting effect that the flavour has on people, including a little old lady and a singing nun. 'Mr Average' also walks into the café and is offered nothing but VIMTO in its many forms. When he asks if anything else is available the waiter sarcastically replies 'No. After all, this is a VIMTO commercial, sir!'

Stills from the VIMTO **'Water Slide' commercial, 1987.**
Adverts for cordial and sparkling VIMTO in 1987, showing zany scenes on a diving board and water slide, were filmed at a water park on the Costa del Sol. They gave new information about product changes. After strong consumer demand and detailed technical research, the nature, though not the taste, of VIMTO changed. Vitamin C and extra fruit juice were added and all artificial colours were removed. 'Max' the bulldog became the company's spokesperson, representing the Britishness of the drink.

Image of Little Mo used on a postcard, shelf wobbler and poster from a specially commissioned piece of artwork by John Farman, 1987.
The illustration won awards in the annual 'Roses Advertising Competition'.

Scenes from the proposed storyboard 'Roly Polys' Diet VIMTO**' colour commercial by Tom Reddy Advertising, Manchester, 1987.**
In the spring of 1987 the new diet version of sparkling VIMTO was launched by the biggest ladies in the business—the Roly Polys. This campaign was created by a new agency founded by Tom Reddy who had been the creative director at Royd's and had already written many of the VIMTO commercial scripts. The 'Polys' were shown dancing their way round an 8ft high can of diet VIMTO, being showered with tinsel in the style of a 1930s' Hollywood musical. The product was presented as a jolly low calorie drink which was fun to drink, rather than being part of a desperately serious diet regime. In 1988 the Roly Poly advert won the Mobius Gold Award from the American Television and Radio Commercials Festival in the soft drinks category, beating both Pepsi-Cola's Michael Jackson and Tina Turner commercials.

The Exciting, Youthful Carbonate

Still from the 'Jet Ski' commercial for sparkling canned VIMTO by Tom Reddy Advertising, Manchester, 1989.
In response to market research, two different approaches to the brand have been adopted to appeal to two very different types of consumer. This light-hearted take-off on the 'boy meets girl on tropical island' theme appeals to the canned carbonate market of out-and-about young people. It also introduced the new logo and can design.

Photographs from the making of the 'Ain't that a Shame' commercial for sparkling canned VIMTO by Tom Reddy Advertising, 1993.
The 1950s' Fats Domino hit *Ain't that a Shame* is used to express concern at just what non-VIMTO drinkers are missing. It challenged them to try the drink to show that they weren't stuck in their ways. It was shown on the relevant television programmes on ITV, Channel 4 and satellite channels, as well as at Warner multiplex cinemas, aiming to reach 82 per cent of the 16–24 year old target audience. The new 'fruity' can design made its debut, along with the young actors, some of whom were given their first television appearance.

The Wholesome Family Cordial

Still from the VIMTO cordial commercial by Tom Reddy Advertising, 1991.

Set on a patio with tennis racquets on the table, a mother prepares a refreshing glass of VIMTO for her children. The advert was designed to appeal to the biggest buyers of VIMTO cordial—mothers, buying for their families to drink at home. A second version of the commercial features the spaniel giving a satirical commentary with the voice of Angus Deayton on the way animals are exploited by advertisers. This widened its appeal to children.

Photographs taken at the making of the 'Cuddly Animals' commercial for VIMTO cordial featuring Victor McGuire, the star from BBC TVs Bread, Tom Reddy Advertising, 1993.

Market research indicated the children's attention was taken by the dog in the 1991 cordial commercial. Now recognised as influential in choice for the shopping trolley, their interest as well as their mother's was catered for. The use 'in true advertising tradition … of some cute cuddly animals' back-fires when the three domestic animals refuse 'to give their views on deliciously different VIMTO cordial.'

Sample pack of VIMTO cordial distibuted through household letterboxes in conjunction with the 'Cuddly Animals' campaign, 1993.

In areas such as East Anglia where VIMTO cordial is still relatively unknown, it was decided to give the cautious householder a taste of VIMTO. Market research indicated that once tasted the product was liked and bought regularly thereafter. A money-off redemption coupon encouraged the consumer to buy a full-size bottle.

The VIMTO Worldbeaters

The collapse of the VIMTO pyramid of cans at G-Mex, Manchester, April 1989.
Under the title 'VIMTO Worldbeaters', a number of challenges to existing world records in the *Guinness Book of Records* have been attempted and achieved. The first success was the building of a giant pyramid consisting of 234,779 empty VIMTO cans, over a period of 40 hours. The Students' Union, in conjunction with the Mechanical Engineering Department of Stockport College of Technology, designed and built the eighth wonder of the world. A *Manchester Evening News* photographer caught the moment when John Nichols placed the last can on top, for the third (and fatal) time, for the benefit of avid press photographers, who had requested repeat performances.

The World's Largest Jigsaw, Armitage Centre, Manchester, March 1991.
The next record was broken by a 1050 m^2 giant jigsaw, designed, painted and laid out by the students of the Faculty of Art and Design at Manchester Polytechnic. The theme was 'VIMTO Through the Ages', and the images were based on three-dimensional tableaux created by the students from hundreds of cans and packaging.

The VIMTO Fountain, London, July 1992.

The pyramidal fountain of 7.75 metres consisting of 16,215 champagne flute glasses successfully overflowed with VIMTO. It broke a world record set in America in 1984. It was done in conjunction with engineering students from Stockport College of Further and Higher Education, who designed the structure with the aid of high-tech computer facilities. The event was filmed by children's BBC's popular *Record Breakers* programme, with Roy Castle helping to get the fountain going.

The biggest working yo-yo in the world re-ascending successfully, Wythenshawe Park, Manchester, August 1993.

The 3.15 metre diameter, 407 kilo plywood laminate yo-yo was worked from a 61 metre crane. The design and construction by students from Stockport College of Further and Higher Education was determined by computer analysis of all variables.

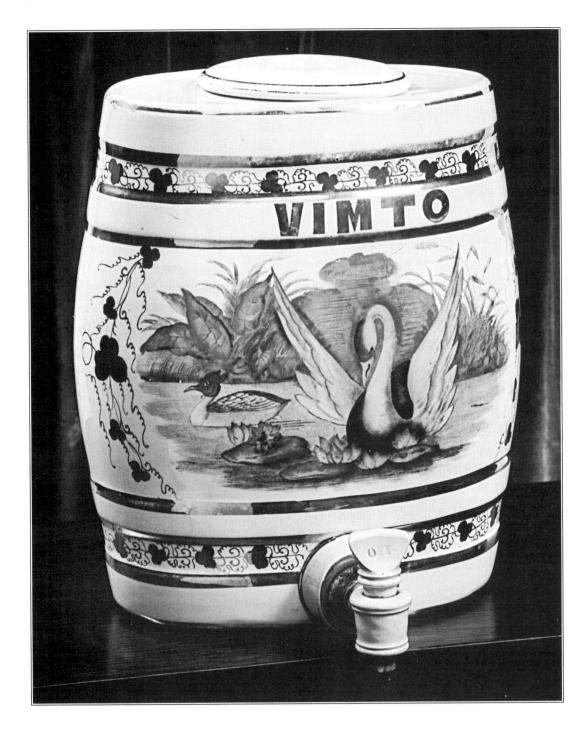

China 'swan design' keg sold by the company for dispensing VIMTO cordial, 1920s.
This example has recently been acquired for the VIMTO Advertising Collection.

3

Smartly Packed and Labelled

PACKAGING AND LABELLING are important in protecting goods from contamination and damage as well as providing the consumer with information. For the marketer, however, they are also essential in maintaining the favours of loyal customers or attracting new ones. This is particularly so today, in the visually competitive world of the supermarket shelf, bereft of manufacturer's point-of-sale material apart from the container and label. The busy shopper or impulse buyer needs to be able to recognise and reach for the brand, rather than asking the shopkeeper. Products should therefore be distinctive, especially when design changes in labelling are made or new packaging is introduced. In the 1920s there were only the carbonated and cordial forms of the VIMTO to label and package, all in glass bottles. Today there are many ways in which the taste of VIMTO is packaged and can be experienced. The risks involved in changing label designs and packaging can be minimised through market research. The company now responds swiftly to the changing taste of consumers, so that the market share for VIMTO can be maintained and expanded.

The early days

There is no visual or written record of the pre-First World War label used for the VIMTO concentrate or 'essence' which was supplied only to temperance bars or herbalists to serve either cold, hot or with the addition of carbonated water. By 1915 order books indicate that it was supplied in one- and two-gallon bottles wrapped in wicker, or six- and twelve-gallon kegs which were returnable. From the early 1920s onwards, however, photographs, illustrations in catalogues, newspaper advertisements and showcards and the labels themselves exist. The retailer could buy china kegs, hot water urns and glasses emblazoned with the VIMTO name. When the concentrate was available for sale directly to the public through the network of franchised bottling companies, sparkling VIMTO appeared in a variety of bottle types and sizes. The unifying factor was the label, which was designed and produced by the Nichols company and supplied free. It became an important means of promoting the drink, reinforcing the point-of-sale and newspaper advertising. Stock labels declared that the drink was 'Bottled by Permit', but the company arranged to have individual labels over-printed with the name and address of the well-established bottling agents. Clear or green glass bottles, sealed with a metal crown cork, flip-top stoppers and Hiram Codd's marble stoppers were all used to retain the effervescence. Children of the first quarter of the century may remember breaking Codd bottles to retrieve the marble.

The number of labels and matching crown corks were in proportion to the amount of concentrate which was supplied, so that the product could not be watered down or mixed with another flavour. The 'beautiful crown corks' were sold for the same price at which the bottler could buy plain ones and were popular with retailers and café owners as they could read the name of the drink on top when bottles were stored in crates at floor level.

The modern look

In more recent years, market research reports and discussions with the marketing department and its advisers have revealed the strategy behind changes in packaging and label design. But until the 1980s, one can only guess at such reasons by using the visual evidence.

The rich, dark blue and red colours, with yellow delineation and white lettering of the label of the first aerated beverage, would have toned well with the dark green bottles displayed on the mahogany shelves of the gaslit herbalist's shops which were the first outlets. The Irish version of the label substituted green for the blue. By 1928, this first label must have begun to appear visually heavy and dated. A cleaner, more linear 'modern' label, with simple lettering on a white background, bordered in gold, was introduced. It was registered in December 1928. It would have suited the cafés and wider range of shops, increasingly lit by electricity, where the drink was now being sold. Clear glass bottles were also becoming more widespread.

In order to ease the customer into the change, a 'Facsimile of Original Label' was

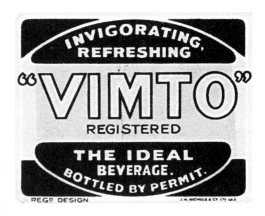

First label for aerated VIMTO supplied free to bottling agents, 1919–28. The marketing messages 'Invigorating', 'Refreshing' and 'The Ideal Beverage' find a place in the design of the label.

incorporated into the new label. More importantly, the block capital lettering with "VIMTO" set in inverted commas was retained. This had become a logo for the company and up until the early 1990s the form 'VIMTO' was used in correspondence and promotional literature in order to highlight the name. The outlined letters of the old label were discarded in favour of red capital lettering in a similar style set against a yellow, shadow effect. However, the use of outlined capital block letters, which was a common way of making a brand name stand out, continued on promotional material well into the 1960s.

The new 1928 carbonate label still harked back to the drink's origins, describing the beverage as 'The Drink of Health' and a 'Fruit Tonic'. Fitness and health became all the rage in the 1930s, so the continuation of this marketing strategy made sense, even though VIMTO was now perceived primarily

Sparkling VIMTO label, 1935–42. The marketing term 'sparkling', which had come into vogue in the 1920s, had been added to the carbonated product label by 1935 to distinguish it a little more from the cordial. As with the first label, either the phrase 'Bottled by Permit' appeared, or the details of an established franchisee were over-printed.

Aerated VIMTO bottle and label, 1928–c. 1935, trade journal insert, 1928 (detail). When labelling changes were made in 1928 the matching neck collar label gave a new opportunity for slogans extolling the virtues of the drink.

as a soft drink rather than a medicinal tonic. The original wording could still be discerned on the miniature label.

By 1926 bottles of VIMTO cordial for drinking at home had been introduced for sale to the public. The first bottle was a simple, dark, wine bottle shape in two sizes. The same bottles were in use for 'Dr Mackenzie's Blood Tonic' and 'The Great Vital Constructor Blood Tonic'. VIMTO cordial was first marketed as a tonic wine with medicinal properties and the packaging reflected this.

The cordial label only had one thing in common with the aerated VIMTO label—a similar script for the brand name in white. It was set against a black background with an eye-catching chequered border. The concentrated syrup in its dark bottle appeared black, so the overall look must have been stylish and mysterious. The label declarations referred to the health benefits of the drink. The bottle was topped with a gold foil, giving an appearance of luxury. The label text was soon amended to describe the drink with the phrase used on contemporary showcards for the carbonate—'Keeps you fit'. It was also supposed to 'Takes away that tired feeling'.

In about 1928 the bottle was changed to the moulded clear glass 'fancy flowered bottle' which was also embossed with a fluted neck. This version of the embossed bottle was

LEFT (top). VIMTO cordial bottles, *c.* 1927–8, either side of a bottle of orange wine cordial. LEFT (bottom). First label for VIMTO cordial, *c.* 1926–7.

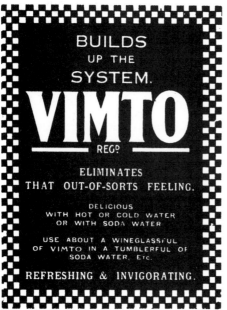

already in use for other fruit cordials and wines in the Nichols range and was unique to the company. The inclusion in the cordial range distinguished by its packaging reflected the growing market for VIMTO as fancy soft drink rather than a herbal tonic. As the packaging became more expensive, it was decided to make the drink more concentrated so that more glasses per bottle could be made up. The drink was soon promoted on the number of glasses of diluted drink it would make, with the 2*s.* 6*d.* pint-and-one-third size making thirty drinks and the 1*s.* 6*d.* two-thirds of a pint size making fifteen drinks. The change in packaging altered the marketing and pricing of the product.

Around 1929 a new cordial label was introduced on similar lines to the carbonate label, which presumably had proved successful. The cordial label was distinguished from that of the carbonate by its tall rectangular shape, the instructions for making up the drink, and the lack of franchise details, as the cordial was only bottled by the Nichols' company. The distinctive gold seal of quality label, with a monogram of the letters 'J N N & Co. Ltd', and the reassurance 'Purity Guaranteed' were added to the neck. This implied a certain prestige and quality. It also gave customers confidence in the drink. A further size of cordial bottle, the small 10*d.* (one third of a pint) size which made eight glasses of cordial was also added to the range.

VIMTO cordial bottle *c.* 1928–9, trade journal insert, 1928 (detail).

VIMTO cordial bottles and display stand, 1932–42. In 1932 a third custom-made embossed bottle was added to the range. Bottling agents were encouraged to distribute the cordial, especially during winter when the

VIMTO decanter (left), sold at Christmas, mid-1930s (gouache); and miniature bottle of VIMTO cordial (right), given away as a sample by retailers, 1930s.

Label issued by the Soft Drinks Industry (War Time) Association Ltd for use for unbranded VIMTO cordial from 1943 to 1947.

When the rationing of raw materials during the Second World War meant that the soft drinks industry came under government control, there were no branded names. From

1943 until 1947, VIMTO shared the description 'Speciality Flavour Cordial' with many other formerly branded fancy drinks. Small undistinguished labels printed in yellow and green

Showcard for sparkling VIMTO and VIMTO cordial, 1948–61. Government labelling restrictions meant that VIMTO finally lost its image as a health tonic.

VIMTO cordial bottle, 1987. The flash 'No tartrazine or Sulphite Preservatives' was added to the neck seal in direct response to consumer concern over the effects of additives in manufactured food and drink. With nearly seventy years behind it, VIMTO could now acquire the description 'Original'. The clipped date indicator and detailed list of ingredients now also gave information to the increasingly aware purchaser. The barcode had to sit unhappily in the label design before the introduction of the back label and, more recently, the wrap-around label.

were issued with the anonymous N.W. 131 code for the Nichols company over-printed.

After the Second World War, the words 'Fruit Tonic', 'Drink of Health' on the main label and 'Invigorating' on the miniature fac-simile label had to be discontinued, because of the new Food Labelling Acts, and instead the drink was described as being a 'Non-Alcoholic Fruit Flavour Cordial' and 'Deli-cious' on the cordial label and simply 'Spark-ling' on the 'pop' bottle. The words changed, but the basic design remained more or less the same until the early 1980s.

Between 1947 and 1986, only the 25.5 fl. oz. cordial bottle size was available. The expensive, embossed glass bottles were dropped in the late 1950s, but the fluted neck was retained. The custom made glass bottle design is the same today, and is also used for the Nichols' blackcurrant cordial and until recently a sarsaparilla.

One-way, recycle or return?

Until the 1950s the unique glass VIMTO cordial bottles, sold all over Britain, were returnable on a deposit basis despite the transport costs involved in getting them back to Manchester. The sparkling form of the drink was bottled by Nichols in returnable glass bottles at the Chorley plant in the 1980s, as the distribution network was much smaller. Many bottling agents, especially those doing household deliveries, ran a returnable system. In general, however, the returnable glass bottle with a deposit is in decline. The rate at which consumers returned bottles for re-use dropped, so manufacturers had to look at other ways of saving money on packaging. The costs in administration, transport and bottle washing also had to be taken into account. Supermarkets in this country are opposed to the sale of carbonated soft drinks in glass bottles, especially the larger heavier ones, because of the danger of breakages. Weight is also a consideration for transport and handling.

Market research indicates that consumers have mixed feelings about glass. They can appreciate the environmental sense of returnable glass bottles and there is an association of quality with the product. On the other hand there is a possible danger when young children get their own drinks. Recent trends in recycling via bottle banks have also supported the one-way bottle system. On the other hand, the energy and environmental costs of producing new glass and the excess refuse of non-recycled bottles would still favour the returnable glass bottle. Manufacturers in the UK are resistant to standardisation because the shape of the bottle is often an integral part of brand recognition and image.

Consumer demand for bulk buying led to the introduction of the larger light-weight plastic packaging. In 1982, sparkling VIMTO was sold in non-returnable 2-litre plastic PET (polyethylene terephthalate). A special flash on the label brought the consumer's attention to the new size. The first ever custom-moulded PET cordial bottle was commissioned by the company in 1987 when the more economical 1.5-litre size was introduced. The distinctive fluted-neck bottle was simply a larger version of the 725ml glass bottle. The body is slightly inset to accommodate the wrap-around label. PET was chosen as a high-quality plastic with clarity and visual appeal to project an up-market image.

The solution to the recycling debate may lie with the new but more expensive returnable and re-usable plastic bottle which can be re-used up to twenty times. PET can be recycled but it needs the support of the bottle manufacturers for schemes to work. In the end it will be a combination of the powers of EC legislation, the bottle manufacturer, the soft drinks industry, the supermarket and the consumer to decide which way the future of glass and plastic packaging will go.

The canned drink

Canned mineral waters were being established in America in the early 1950s. Initially they were produced to attract sales from retailers who were in areas such as beach resorts, where broken glass was a hazard and local bye-laws prohibited the sale of glass bottled drinks. They were tapered in shape in order to be reminiscent of a bottle and so ease consumers into the new form of packaging. From a transport point of view, it was found that twice the amount could be carried in cans compared with bottles.

The advantages of canned drinks were eventually recognised in the United Kingdom. Their introduction went hand in hand with changes in retailing. Grocery stores and supermarkets found them easier to handle in bulk; they are unbreakable; and they stack and display well. The consumer liked their portability and the fact that they are non-returnable. In 1963 they represented 4 per cent by volume of the total soft drinks market. Today they account for over 65 per cent.

VIMTO was first filled in steel 'tins' or cans in about 1964 by Stotherts Ltd. It was a heavy can which had to be opened with the aid of a triangular steel opener until the ring-pull was introduced in the late 1960s. Ring-pulls became an environmental hazard but the issue has been partially addressed by the introduction from 1989 of the 'retain-end' or 'stay on tab' types. The new design is also more 'user-friendly' and easier to open. Since the mid-1970s, cans have gradually become thinner and lighter and made in two pieces rather than three. The '206' diameter necked-in profile can for VIMTO was introduced in 1987. Until 1993, the cans were made of steel, but the new 'fruity' can design worked best with the

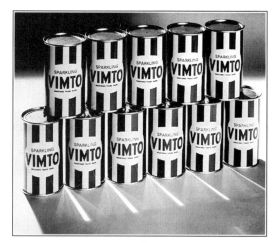

The first VIMTO can, 1964. Opened by a can opener, and made from heavy steel, the first cans did not have the portability associated with this type of packaging today.

reflective qualities of aluminium. Both steel and aluminium cans can be recycled, the former by magnetic extraction at refuse depots, the latter through collection campaigns and recycling banks.

Trends in canning include the popular 440ml can of VIMTO with '⅓ Extra Free'. This is introduced into areas where the drink is not so well known, to encourage new customers. It also rewards 'heavy drinkers' in established areas. In April 1994 150ml 'fun-size' cans were launched. As well as being a handier size for children, they also introduced new users to the brand by way of a lower purchase price.

Responding to the market

The first VIMTO can design in 1964, with its thick red, blue and white vertical stripes, bore no relationship to the cordial or sparkling

The VIMTO range, 1982. The plasticised all-round label on the 1.5-litre glass bottle and the new 2-litre PET bottle were introduced in 1982, when attention was being focused away from the export market towards the home trade.

bottle labels apart from the block capital lettering. This is because it was decided that a new form of packaging should have an equally modern, youthful design. The striped pattern was distinctive and eye-catching. The colour scheme and design reflected the Union Jack and drew attention to the Britishness of the beverage, as opposed to the increasing number of American imports. The drink was simply described as 'sparkling' and gave no clue to its flavour or benefits. The inverted commas around the brand name were also dropped.

In 1982 this bold striped design was carried over on to the first large 1.5-litre PET bottle of sparkling VIMTO in conjunction with Corona, who were bottling and distributing VIMTO in the South. The plasticised label was a continuous 'All-rounder' and came already fixed to the bottle. New printing techniques gave a boldness to the colour. The design was the same from every angle and solved the

Bottle of sparkling VIMTO with promotional on-pack offers, 1986. For the first time the label design had to be compromised to accommodate 'flash' announcements which informed customers of special offers.

problem of correct shelf-stacking. The same design in different colours was used for the Sunglora Cola and Lemonade labels, giving a unified 'family' feel to the products as well as making more visual impact on the display shelf.

As in the 1920s, the cordial and carbonated versions of the drink had distinct labelling linked only by the name 'VIMTO' in capital letters. The striped design was also introduced on the labels of the franchised bottles of sparkling VIMTO. A smaller but buoyant number of bottling agents continue to bottle

VIMTO in a variety of shapes and sizes, with
labelling as the unifying factor. Printing of
labels is now the responsibility of the agents,
but, in order to retain the brand image, all of
them must conform to a standard design laid
down by the company

The simple, uncluttered, but uninform-
ative can design of the 1960s had become
visually hectic by the 1987. The brief description 'Fruit Flavour Drink' had been added in
the early 1980s and the text had been separ-
ated from the stripes by an a double ellipse.
In 1986 the description was changed to
'Mixed Fruit Juice Drink' to satisfy labelling
legislation when the fruit content was increased. Max the Bulldog sporting a striped
top and declaring VIMTO to be 'The Grrreat
British Drink' also appeared. The original
idea behind the red, white and blue stripes
had been extended. In 1987 Max's speech
bubble gave information about changes to the
product. In response, sales of cans in 1987
increased by 30 per cent. Max the Bulldog
became a logo for the company and appeared
on other forms of packaging. The cordial was
described as tasting 'Grrreat hot'. It became a
'fun' way of relaying customer information.

Once this new image and information
about the drink had been established it was
decided that the time was right to change the
packaging. Extensive meetings were held
with the external advisors to the company,
Tom Reddy Advertising, Maley Design &
Advertising and market research companies.
Detailed surveys with thirteen- to seventeen-
year-olds in 1989 compared the striped can
design with four new designs, which incorporated the capital letter name logo in its

The VIMTO range in 1987 featuring 'Max the
Bulldog', who informed customers that VIMTO
'contains fruit juice and Vitamin C' and 'no
artificial colour'.

ellipse. The basically 1960s design did not fare
well. The stripes were judged to be too
simple and did not give the idea of a refreshing drink. The block letters, which had been
synonymous with the beverage for so long,
were now declared old-fashioned and heavy.
The bulldog character was deemed to be
childish by southern drinkers new to the
product, although he was popular with regular drinkers. The elements liked best in the
four trial designs were incorporated into two
new can designs which were presented in
further market research. The preferred design, which aimed to introduce VIMTO to
teenagers, was set against an up-to-date
metallic electric blue. Silver bubbles gave the

Poster and press advert introducing the new can pack, 1987.

The VIMTO range in 1991, with the diagonal script logo as the unifying factor.

idea of a refreshing drink. The VIMTO name was changed to an informal upper and lower case script in a metallic red, set against white, sweeping diagonally across the can. The writing style reflected that of many young people, and research indicated that the radical change in script, colour and overall design was acceptable, especially amongst people not familiar with the product. The packaging was supported by a new, humorous television commercial with a 'boy and girl meet on the beach' theme also aimed at raising the age profile of the drinkers of canned VIMTO. There was no conformity with the previous can apart from a miniature version of the old name style in the ellipse which was incorpor-

ated to ease identification. The phrase 'The Original Unique Taste' surrounded the miniature ellipse to tell people that although it was a brand-new can the drink was well established. A poster and trade advert acknowledging 'the stripes have gone but the taste goes on' showed the old can peeling back to reveal the new design. The ellipse label with the old name style was dropped in 1992 when the new design was established in its own right.

Change across the range

The new can with its diagonal script logo was an immediate success, so it was decided to abandon the block lettering across the whole range of VIMTO products. The can design of the 'diet' version was very similar to the standard version but set against a white background.

The sparkling label version of the standard drink adopted the blue ground with a white pattern of bubbles and diagonal stripes, with the scripted VIMTO letters in red.

The cordial label, however, took up the new script but retained its overall design elements and colour scheme of red, yellow, blue, black and gold on white. Changes had already been made to the cordial range. The 'Purity Guaranteed' neck seal label had gradually been more economically incorporated into the front body label. It also acquired the new scripted logo rather than the updated monogram 'J N N Plc'. The 'facsimile of original label' had been moved to the lower part of the label and given less prominence. It was actually replaced for a few years when the barcode took its place before the back label was introduced. The changes were small, in order to ensure visual continuity for the customer when searching for the product. This is an important consideration in an age when supermarkets continually move products around from above eye level, to eye level, to children's level and to foot level.

However, further market research in 1990 revealed that the quality seal was seen as making the drink appear to be alcoholic and the 1920s' label was often described as a 'tobacco tin'. It was a point of historical interest, but had long ago lost its purpose as a visual transition. It was also found that different regions perceived the label in different ways. Unlike advertising, which can be targeted on a regional basis, the label has to appeal to people in all areas. In the North West it was found that a household would buy VIMTO, a bottle of blackcurrant, and one other flavour, to cope with the family's taste preferences. In areas such as East Anglia, in contrast, the drink was mainly remembered as a bottle of 'pop' from the 1950s, and VIMTO was seen as just another blackcurrant drink. In these areas people needed more visual information on the label to indicate that VIMTO is a complex and intriguing drink rather than a simple, single flavour. It was decided to carry out another survey to 'improve the appeal of VIMTO cordial amongst southern buyers whilst not alienating existing northern buyers'. The current label and four new candidate designs by Maley Design were presented to mothers of children who were 'current' or 'lapsed or never buyers' in two regions, the North West and southern England. All the new designs incorporated the new scripted logo which was by now well established in the customer's mind. For the first time they also hinted at some of the ingredients of VIMTO, namely the fruit. This would take a little of the mystery away for the initiated, but would encourage the less in-the-know cordial drinker to try it. The designs were evaluated on their brand image. The new label also had to be both appealing and eye-catching. It was intended that 'VIMTO' should still be recognised as the one unique flavour—rather than a line extension whereby one brand name is used for a variety of flavours.

One design came out as an overall success, especially with the 'lapsed or never buyers'. It gave the impression of a fruity drink for all the family with distinctive and noticeable packaging. Contrasting with the bright blue dynamic design of the carbonate range, the proposed cordial label had a traditional oval shape and incorporated a little historical information in the form of a gold banner declaring the drink to be 'Original since 1908'. The border introduced in 1928 was retained,

Trial VIMTO 1.5-litre wrap-around cordial label, July–September 1992.

but the small facsimile label and 'Purity Guaranteed' seal were dropped. When asked why the design was suitable for the brand, respondents frequently claimed that the taste went with the label. The new label was introduced to selected supermarkets in southern England in July 1992. Sales at comparable outlets were set against those of the old label, and although there was no dramatic increase in sales of the new label, the results gave the company enough confidence to introduce it nationwide. The design was amended slightly, and has been well received by both loyal and new customers. The design was carried across to the new low-sugar version of the cordial which was launched in 1993. Silver replaces the gold and the background is white, rather than the VIMTO black on the standard cordial, which blends with the full bottle.

With the installation of a new cordial bottling line at the Wythenshawe factory in 1993, both the .725-litre and the 1.5-litre bottles now have the design advantage of the wrap-around label.

Trade leaflet for Low Sugar vimto, 1993, by Maley Design & Advertising. No actual artwork exists for most of the company's publications today because the background, imagery and lettering are all computer-generated.

The 'fruity' can

With the decision to reveal some of the fruit ingredients on the cordial label in early 1993 came the latest qualitative market research with teenagers on the striped blue can design. It was compared with a variant on the stripe and three new 'fruity' cans. Having been hailed as fashionable, desirable and exciting in 1989, it was now described as being 'dull' and 'dated'. It gave no obvious clues as to the fruit content of the drink. The consumer is now aware of the difference between fruit-juice-based drinks and the less desirable fruit-flavoured carbonates on the market. Although the taste of VIMTO was enjoyed, the true fruitiness of the drink was not fully appreciated. It was also found that the packaging did not project a 'character' or 'personality' of the brand. The brand was drunk for taste alone, not for the advertising or the imagery. As the bulk of canned drinks are consumed by young people in public, in the company of friends, the can has now become a fashion accessory. The image and packaging, as well as the taste, have to be acceptable and up-to-date.

It was also revealed that proposed straplines such as 'Taste the Difference' were misleading as they implied that the taste had changed. It appears that the pack carries the main overall message and that individual slogans are overlooked or disregarded by teenagers.

The three designs were then tested on a quantitative basis with thirteen- to eighteen-year-old 'users' and 'non users' in the North and South of England. The aim was to establish the preferred design, the likelihood to buy and the awareness, usage and brand image of VIMTO against other main brands. Consistency with the preferred design and reaction to taste were also checked.

The final can designs to emerge combined the best elements of each test design. The 'Diet' version is distinguished from the standard blue can by its silver background and 'Diet' and 'Low Calorie' flashes. They both satisfy the marketer's requirements of giving the impression of a fruity, different and intriguing drink in a fun, trendy, colourful and eye-catching can which teenagers 'would be happy to be seen with'. The use of transparent inks on a highly reflective aluminium can added to the visual appeal. The design was carried across to the bottles of sparkling VIMTO.

Other forms of packaging

The other form in which vimto is sold is in the ready-to-drink still version, packaged in the sealed plastic cup since 1972 and the handy Tetra Brik since 1982. The RTD or ready-to-drink cordial market was revolutionised by the Tetra Pak company of Sweden has been the fastest-growing sector of the soft drinks market. Being lightweight, safe and easy to open and store, these containers are popular with both children and parents. The Tetra Brik is also popular with adults on motorway and train journeys, as well as with those taking part in outdoor sports and leisure pursuits. Consumption is all-year-round, not just as an immediate summer drink. The 'single-shot ready-to-drink multipack' of six 200ml cups was introduced in 1990. The new scripted VIMTO logo in red with a yellow drop-shadow was also added to these two RTD forms of packaging. Previously combining elements from both the can and cordial label, the range was given its own distinctive illustration in the form of the 'VIMTO Wave' in 1990. It was designed to appeal to the five- to twelve-year-old. The coloured design was carried to the corrugated tray holding Tetra Briks and the cardboard packaging surrounding the cups. The 'Vimto Wave' worked particularly well on the latter, with the visual continuity between the cup and the pack. In 1993, the packaging has been redesigned once again to bring it in line with the 'fruity' image on the sparkling form of the drink.

The trend for canned drinks sales in supermarkets is also for multi-pack sales. Environmental concerns over the addition of extra packaging have been expressed. However, at the moment the convenience of transport and shelf-stacking for the supermarket, and economical bulk buying and convenience for the consumer seem to take precedence.

Unified only by the name and the scripted diagonal logo in red, the cordial, ready-to-drink and sparkling forms of VIMTO are seen as different product versions of the same brand. However, each version has its own distinctive design elements and style according to its usage and appeal. The markets have now been clearly identified and the brand, the nature of its packaging and its labelling will continue to satisfy each sector. But underlying all this, the unique VIMTO taste, which is really what counts, will continue to intrigue and delight in whatever form it is contained, labelled and consumed.

VIMTO packaging, 1994. The diverse forms of VIMTO are united by the scripted logo in red, and the fruit imagery.

LEFT. Trade leaflet, 1930s.
VIMTO was promoted as an
all-the-year-round drink,
thirst-quenching in summer
and warming in winter. It was
associated with both winter and
summer sporting activities.

BELOW. A Whit Week holiday
treat in Benllech Bay, Anglesey,
1950.

4

Sold Wherever Mineral Waters Are Obtainable

BEFORE the First World War VIMTO was only available in herbalists' shops which had an area set aside for serving drinks, or in temperance bars. Here it was on sale as a healthy non-alcoholic tonic, but it could not be found elsewhere. After the war, when bottling agents across the nation were encouraged to take up the VIMTO agency in their areas, it became more widely available in a portable form. The general increase in the availability and popularity of soft drinks in the twentieth century reflects a much broader social picture. As standards of living rose, consumers had more spare money for non-essential items, such as VIMTO, and more time to spend on leisure pursuits which were enhanced by the consumption of sweet fruit beverages. To the basic negative 'need' of avoiding discomfort by quenching the thirst was added the positive luxury of 'want' in seeking pleasure by choosing and quaffing a soft drink.

The rise in consumerism

In America between 1890 and 1930 the large and increasingly wealthy population and the protected national market began to sustain the sales of standardised products marketed by large corporations. The rise in consumerism went hand in hand with the expansion of mass production and the branding of products. New processed convenience foods, such as breakfast cereals; forms of packaging to preserve foods, such as tins; and consumer durables for the home were all rapidly developed and promoted. In Britain, too, in the inter-war period, a wide range of branded products in colourful packaging became more cheaply and more freely available at the corner shop. As consumer spending power increased it became possible to choose goods for reasons other than price, and this meant that a complex dialogue between manufacturer and customer began to develop.

The brand

The brand identity, in particular, provides a direct communication between the manufacturer and the customer. Consistent quality in a standardised, hygienic and recognisable packaging, without danger of adulteration or substitution by the wholesaler or shopkeeper, gave the consumer confidence and trust in a particular named product. Repeat purchases made with confidence and without too much consideration became far more likely. Advertising gives a personality and an image, which helps to differentiate the brand, and which the customer can recognise. The brand identity gives added value to the basic function and appearance of the product or service. Today, with an increasingly international market dominated by large corporations, 'global' brands are in the process of becoming bland in their appeal. In soft drinks, the image of the brand, as reflected by advertising and packaging, can be as important as taste, quality or value for money.

'Most of our people have never had it so good'

Although many of the well-known brands today were established early in the century, it was not until the 1950s in Britain that consumerism became a significant feature of everyday life. Particularly after 1955, there was a striking increase in the affluence and spending power of the community. There was full employment, and the average real earnings of an industrial worker increased by 20 per cent between 1951 and 1958, so that most ordinary families could now consider buying a washing machine, refrigerator or car. After the necessities had been paid for, there was cash left for the luxuries. Commercial television revealed a wonderful world of commodities which could be bought, or at least desired for the future.

The boom in soft drinks

By 1953, when sugar was finally de-rationed, there had already been an enormous five-fold increase over pre-war levels in the consumption of soft drinks. This was partially created by the Ministry of Food wartime regulations. The dearth of sweet eatables and drinks for a decade created pent-up demand. During the war, the encouragement given to concentrated drinks aided the cordial manufacturers. The issuing of 'National Orange Juice' for children and expectant mothers developed the habit for soft drinks. Travel in foreign parts, where drinking with meals was more common than at home, was another factor. The increasing availability of domestic refrigerators, which allowed stocks of cold drinks to be kept 'on tap', and the higher price of beer, were also conducive to the market. The cinema saw a great increase in the sales of soft drinks, alongside ice creams. The growth of snack bars, milk bars, and travelling refreshment vans, all selling soft drinks, provided further outlets.

The drinking of sparkling soft drinks was also associated with the fashion for all things American which had intensified during and after the war. Coca-Cola was seen by some trade experts as a potential threat, but most decided that it was too sickly and sweet for the British palate, especially when drunk at room temperature. In France, however, a violent campaign against the American 'Coca-Colarisation' of Europe almost led the National Assembly to ban its sale in 1950.

The pursuit of leisure

The rise in consumerism was inextricably associated with the increase in time and some cases money spent on leisure activities, a trend which had been developing since the end of the nineteenth century. Between the two world wars, the increase in real wages, and shorter and more regular working hours

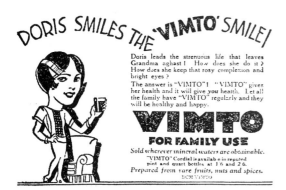

Newspaper advertisement, 1928.

meant that ordinary people could participate in the wide variety of sports and fun pursuits organised on a voluntary or commercial basis. Activities could be pursued for the sake of enjoyment and fitness rather than just being a rest from work. Improvements in public transport and the wider ownership of bicycles, motorbikes and cars meant that people could explore the world beyond their immediate neighbourhood.

Unmarried young people in their late teens and early twenties, who were working but still living at home, had a certain amount of affluence and freedom in the towns and cities of Britain. Relationships between men and women became more open and independent by the 1920s. Gradually young women of all classes could go to the cinema, café or dance hall with a boyfriend without their parents objecting, though most recall a 10 o'clock curfew.

They exercised their consumer choice in the purchase of clothes, magazines, cosmetics and soft drinks and in their attendance at cinemas, cafés, dance halls, milk bars, ice cream parlours and sporting activities. Many of the products and leisure activities were aimed at young people. Most of the sparkling VIMTO point-of-sale material dating from the inter-war period depicts young, attractive men and women participating in sporting activities or refreshing themselves. But then, as today, the world of advertising is predominantly inhabited by the youthful and appealing. The newspaper advertisements described single women such as 'Doris' who, with the help of sparkling VIMTO, led 'the strenuous life that leaves Grandma aghast!' However, they also depicted every other age and class in the country. VIMTO cordial was marketed for economical family use at home, as it is today, but sparkling VIMTO was meant to be consumed by everyone—not just the out-and-about people in their teens.

It was not until the 1950s that the phenomenon of the 'teenager' as a distinct and novel phase of life was recognised by contemporary sociologists and indeed young people themselves. The more widespread use of market research ensured that teenage products could be fully marketed and advertised or new products and services could be especially created. For VIMTO, however, it was not until 1987 that a distinct advertising and packaging strategy for the canned sparkling form, aimed at the teenage market, was formulated.

Health and fitness

During the 1930s, when the first craze for 'keep-fit' and healthy living was at its height, VIMTO refreshed and restored many a flagging sportswoman or man. It was described as a

"a Pleasant Interlude"

"Ping . . . ping ! Vantage out ! . . . ping . . . Game and set ! And now something to drink . . . I'd love some VIMTO please."

Of course. Few drinks are as cooling and delicious as VIMTO. Few with the same health properties as VIMTO. One asks for it automatically.

And the children clamour for VIMTO. As it is so good for them, you'll know what to do now.

Drink it as you would any good mineral water. It is sold wherever such is obtainable at usual high class mineral water prices.

Vimto Cordial is also obtainable for family use in 1 6 and 2 6 bottles.

J. N. NICHOLS & CO., LTD., Manchester, S.W.

SPARKLING
VIMTO
THE IDEAL SUMMER DRINK

Newspaper advertisement, 1929. The soft drink gives an excuse for socialising between matches.

'sporty drink' and many of the advertisements depicted the most popular pursuits of the day, such as tennis, golf, football and cricket. It also became a focal point for the social aspect of sporting activities.

The cult of the healthy, athletic body was combined with a renewed love of the countryside, contrasting with life in the polluted industrialised towns. It was an inexpensive, sociable and classless form of exercise. Hikers Leagues and Clubs were founded and large groups of ramblers would set off for the day, sometimes catching a 'Mystery Express' train to an unknown destination. Shorts, open-neck shirts and berets were the dress for the

expedition, and the obligatory rucksack might contain a bottle of VIMTO and some cottage cheese for sustenance. Overnight stays could be made at the growing number of youth hostels—the Youth Hostels Association was founded in 1930.

The modern craze for 'outside air' and sunshine was also satisfied by cycling. Cafés in the countryside and on the outskirts of big towns would encourage cyclists to stop and refresh themselves. The steep, winding road above Pwllheli, beyond Four Crosses on the Lleyn Peninsula is unofficially called 'VIMTO Valley' a nickname which probably dates from the time when cyclists would stop at a house where drinks were served, and which had an advertisement for VIMTO. Sunday schools sometimes ran day-long charabanc outings into the countryside, introducing children from the cities to the pleasures of long grass, wild flowers and farm animals.

The 1920s and '30s also saw the building of stylish outdoor swimming complexes known as lidos. Swimming and sunbathing became part of the healthy life. Seaside towns continued to be popular and were the destination for many workers from the industrialised northern towns during Wakes Weeks, when entire businesses would close down for the annual holiday.

The milk bar

The milk bar was the great hope of the temperance movement in the late 1930s. Young people on a 'keep fit' ritual would gather to sip a VIMTO milk shake, either hot or cold, or other milk cocktails such as

Showcard, 1920s. The cardboard was textured and coloured to look like gold-embossed brown leather.

'Golden Gleam', 'Sunset Ray' or a 'Purple Kick'. The first milk bar in Bolton, for example, opened in 1937. It was described in Mass-Observation's *The Pub and the People: A Worktown Study* published in 1943. Although it was the setting for 'pub-like' social groups, the milk bar could not sustain all-evening drinking sessions because of both the cost and the filling nature of milk. It was found that, after being turned out of the pub at 10.30 p.m., people went on to the milk bar for a milk shake, soup and Horlicks. Some brewers did, however, feel threatened by the milk bar alternative, and considered selling milk shakes together with alcohol to bring trade back again.

The public house

Despite VIMTO's origin as a temperance beverage, it is regarded by many as an excellent mixer for alcoholic drinks. The company itself promoted it as such during the 1930s. Today, a 'Macki Vim'—a Mackeson Stout and sparkling VIMTO—is still popular in the Midlands, and a 'Scrumpy Tan'—cider mixed

with VIMTO—is a Somerset favourite. When mixed with Guinness, the drink is called 'A Pink Velvet'. A hot VIMTO with rum is a sure winter warmer or 'remedy' for a cold.

The custom-built public house of the 1920s and '30s, situated in the new suburbs or on the new by-pass roads, catered increasingly for women. However, even children of the 1950s, particularly in the Midlands, remember sitting on the pub step with a bottle of sparkling VIMTO and a packet of crisps, waiting for their parents. Many large pubs today welcome families by providing special rooms, playgrounds, a children's menu and high chairs. Smaller pubs, however, are still restricted by licensing laws and are reluctant to allow children in the bar areas. VIMTO is still available in pubs in regions where long-standing agreements with local bottlers exist, such as in the Midlands. Cabana Soft Drinks are gradually installing post-mix draught vending machines in pubs and other leisure venues, providing a range of flavours.

'Fish and chips and a Vimto, please'

Individuals disagree over which food goes best with VIMTO. A packet of crisps, pie and peas, chopped herring sandwiches and a curry have all been cited. Fashion designer Bruce Oldfield has been quoted in the press as saying that whenever he wants to remember his childhood in Yorkshire, he seeks out mushy peas, black pudding, mashed potatoes and VIMTO. Jasper Carrot refers to 'a Wagon Wheel and a VIMTO' in his Midlands Airport sketch. The Bee Gees remember hot pies and

ABOVE. Joanne's fish and chip shop, Borough Road, Altrincham, Cheshire, displaying red and white glass window tiles, 1991. The shop is the oldest in the area and was established by Alexander Perris, 'fried fish dealer' in 1902. By the 1900s the fish and chip shop had become a welcome sight in most working-class areas. Deep-sea trawlers and the use of ice provided a supply of cheap Icelandic cod.

BELOW. The Whit Walk of St Bartholomew's Church, Salford, mid-1920s.

VIMTO from their youth. There is no doubt however, that fish and chips is one of the most popular accompaniments, as described by Victoria Wood in her song *At the Chippy*, 'I could drink it by the crate!'

The Whit Walks

At Whitsuntide, in and around Manchester, Sunday Schools, Church Groups and Chapels would do their walk of witness around the local streets, usually accompanied by a band. The Protestant and Catholic processions were held at different times over the holiday week-end. Everyone dressed up in their finest clothes. Children were taken to show off their finery to friends and relatives, who would pop a few coins in their pockets. The walks finished at their respective schools or places of worship, for refreshments. After-

wards, there were often traditional games such as the three-legged race on the local open spaces. The official programmes for the Whit Walks regularly featured the advert 'Don't forget "VIMTO"'.

The showcard advertising VIMTO appeared in the bars, shops and cafés where it was sold.

Club journals and the cinema programmes, Whit walks and sporting events all had relevant reminders of the drink's availability. VIMTO drinkers could find themselves or their aspirations reflected, with glamour or with humour, in the brand image of a fun, healthy drink.

A merry troupe in Bolton, 1923.

The Temperance Bar

Mr and Mrs Robert Whalley and their daughter Annie outside their temperance bar on the Manchester Road, mid-1920s.

VIMTO was served in temperance bars, grocers, tobacconists and confectioners, who set up simple rooms with a bar, table and chairs. They sold only non-alchoholic drinks and were encouraged by temperance and church groups. They were well supported by the local community as they provided warm, comfortable surroundings in which women and children could feel safe, unlike the public house.

Cinema advert for Elliot's Temperance Bar, Sheffield, using the image of a tennis girl showcard.
Temperance bars were also very popular with sporting groups, especially tennis clubs who would get together after a match.

'The temperance bar, that was another place where we could spend a comfortable two hours, and without any detriment to our character. We could go and sit in that temperance bar, buy a VIMTO and probably a waffle; they'd put jam on it for yer. For tuppence tha could sit there for an hour or two; chatting and not getting into any mischief. Now, that's another thing that's gone by the board.'
Looking Back at the **Bolton Area (1983)**

YES SIR, IT'S
VIMTO!
The TONIC DRINK
with the Fine flavour.
Obtainable at all Temperance Bars.

"One good tip deserves another!"

Artwork for a cinema advert by Ball, 1928 (pencil and water colour). Temperance bars in gentlemen's clubs and hotels for respectable travellers were well established by the 1920s.

Mr Waddington in the last temperance bar in England—Herbal Health, Rawtenstall, 1990. By the 1950s, the temperance bar could still be found, but the signs were usually pre-war. Herbal Health, however, is a thriving business owned by Mr and Mrs Waddington who still prepare, sell and serve a range of herbal remedies, tonics and temperance drinks.

'My sister and I, then 14, had the job of helping in the canteen and VIMTO was the only drink. Gallons were swigged weekly at the club and many were consumed at "The Temp" [the Victoria Avenue Temperance Bar] after the club closed. It was really an extension of the club's social gathering.'
Patricia Hayes remembering the youth centre in Higher Blackley in the 1940s (1991).

A Hot VIMTO at the Herbalists

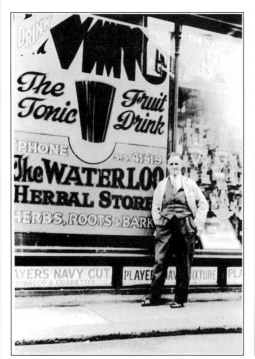

The Waterloo Herbal Stores, Blackpool, 1920s.
The herbalists or 'herb shop' was a familiar sight on many high streets until the late 1940s. Many would have a few tables and chairs set out and serve mineral waters and tonic drinks. A glass of VIMTO, which was promoted as a healthy tonic, would cost 1*d*. The Nichols company would help meet the costs of individual signs advertising VIMTO.

'The herbalist, temperance bar or "hot drink shop" was the only shop where children could go in and sit down on the benches or chairs and have a drink. In summer, coming home from the local parks, we always called in for a cool VIMTO before going home for our tea. In winter we would call in after having been to the cubs or scouts meeting and sit drinking VIMTO very hot.'
Albert Heaveside on Miles Platting in the 1920s (1991).

'There was a herbalist called Pickles on Alexandra Road, Moss Side. It always seemed cool, quiet and mysterious and as a special treat I was allowed to sit on a high stool and have a hot VIMTO in winter and cold VIMTO in summer. I used to buy camomile flowers there which I would boil, then rinse my hair in the water to keep it fair.'
Dorothy Bradbury recalling the 1930s (1991).

Showcard, late 1920s.
The gentleman's hand offers a glass which was often used to serve hot or cold VIMTO before World War Two.

A glass 'tot', early 1920s.

The concentrate would have been dispensed by a plunger or taken from a china barrel and measured by a small glass known as a 'tot'. Hot water (usually from a metal urn) or cold water was added. An effervescence could be given to the drink by a simple soda siphon or a more elaborate soda fountain. Herbalists would make their own drinks up or combine flavours. The Nichols company supplied china barrels, metal urns, soda fountains, 'tots' and glasses.

Cinema advert, late 1920s.

Poem by Madge Owen written for the company's 75th anniversary, 1983.

Billy Owen was a lad in Salford who used to gather nettles with a friend every Saturday. They would take them to the local herbalist shop and were paid with a glass of VIMTO. It was in a herbalist shop, by gaslight, that Billy later proposed to his wife, Madge Owen, over a glass of hot VIMTO.

VIMTO Days

I often think back in many ways
To the time folk called the poverty days,
When as a child with others I knew,
We'd often run errands for a copper or two.

Off we would go with a skip and a hop
To buy a VIMTO at the herbalist's shop.
If one hadn't coppers, girl or lad,
We shared out between us the little we had.

Then I started courting—a bit early, you see,
A lovely lad, as shy as could be,
He never said much, not forward at all;
It was his dark curly hair that made me fall!

One night as we sat in our favourite shop,
Sipping our VIMTO—it was piping hot—
He suddenly said with a brazen smile,
"Let's get married!" I was stumped for a while.

It made me say yes—in a bewildered tone,
We hadn't got the price of our tram fare home!
Perhaps the hot VIMTO hit the spot—
It certainly started him talking a lot!

There are many have memories of those bygone days
When poverty reigned in so many ways,
But our special memory stands out a mile
And when we recall it we both have to smile.

How fitting it was that a Salford lad
Popped the question over a VIMTO he had
To a girl who as a child to buy VIMTO would hop—
And it happened in a Salford herbalist's shop.

The Corner Shop

A grocer's shop, 1937.
This photograph was used by *The Daily Herald* in June 1937 with the caption 'It is not the retailer's fault when the housewife cannot buy all she would like to', illustrating an article on the rising cost of living, which was blamed on the government.

Until the Second World War small local shops, often situated at the end of a terrace, sold the food most people needed. Mass production meant that a wide range of branded products in colourful packaging became cheaper and more available. Biscuits, rice, sugar and dried fruits were still sold loose.

Food was bought almost daily, often 'on tick' (credit). Grocers stocked VIMTO cordial and sparkling VIMTO, along with medications the company sold. Nowadays, large impersonal supermarkets seem more suited to most shoppers' needs. Many take credit cards, thus still selling goods 'on tick'.

Boys from the Macclesfield area enjoying their purchase from the corner shop, 1960.
One sports a yellow and red VIMTO badge given to him by the shopkeeper.

'A vivid memory I have is about a sweet shop near the VIMTO factory in Ayres Road. Not only could we buy our penny chews and two ounces of cinder toffee, but the proprietress made penny and twopenny VIMTO iced lollies. Also, part of the shop was partitioned from the main area. It had frosted etched glass on the door and inside there was a polished wooden counter and a round wrought-iron pub table and chairs. In there you could buy hot or cold VIMTO to drink sitting in this cosy room. My husband used to go into this shop as well and we both recall a glass water geyser with VIMTO in red emblazoned on it. The shop had a cosy, safe atmosphere which is very rare today.'
Ann Edgar recalling the 1950s (1991).

The Café

Newspaper advert, 1929.

'O'Donnell's or Brown's café must have been the rendezvous of hundreds of courting couples in the twenties and early thirties. Over a hot blackcurrant juice or a VIMTO, buying a fourpenny or sixpenny ice cream, a flapper could feel as sophisticated as the heroines of *Peg's Paper* and a masher, even though he might be toiling over a ledger in a cotton mill office the next day, on a Sunday evening could know himself to be as smart, handsome and desirable to the girls as any Valentino or Navarro. Dreams were cheap in the twenties, but then they always were.'
Kay Davenport, *Some Oldham Times* **(1991).**

Rotating showcard, early 1930s.

Market Square Café, Market Drayton, Shropshire, 1960.
Unlike today, where it is impractical for sales representatives to approach owners directly, most cafés until the 1960s served VIMTO.

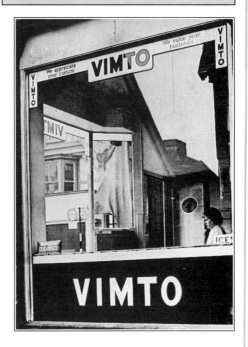

'The Joys of Dancing'

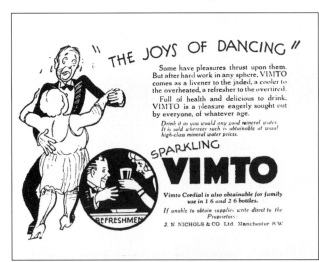

Newspaper advert, 1932.
Dancing to the profusion of dance bands at a variety of venues was enjoyed by most people. The tunes had become popular through the gramophone, wireless and cinema. In 1928 Al Jolson's *Sonny Boy* from *The Singing Fool* was played by every band and barrel organ across the country. Professional couples would sometimes demonstrate the waltz, slow foxtrot, quickstep and the tango. Tea-dances in the mid-afternoon were also popular with women and the unemployed.

'It wouldn't do to go out for a drink of beer, as it wouldn't have been nice to hold a girl in your arms for a dance and breathe the smell of beer in her face. Everything was done prim and proper. Christmas and New Year was the highlight of the year. Everyone dressed up in their finery, the girls in lovely dresses and silver or gold shoes.'
Albert Heaviside on the 1930s (1991).

Betty Burden, 16 (in the striped dress) enjoys a VIMTO with her boyfriend in the canteen at a local Saturday night dance, Birmingham, 1951.
Picture Post photographer Bert Hardy recorded the day-to-day routine of Betty, a hairdresser, for an article on the lives of ordinary working girls in big industrial towns.

Detail of a late 1950s' showcard showing an alluring girl in evening dress, which claimed that 'Sparkling VIMTO' was 'Delicious and Exhilarating'.

'You were boppers in those days. You wore your white socks with 'be-bop' on and your big skirts … it was a café around a juke box with a VIMTO for as long as you wanted—we weren't moved!' **Dorothy Carroll quoted in the press on her teenage memories of Hartlepool in the 1950s (1987).**

'Makes the Cream of Ices'

Cover of a booklet costing 2s. 6d. containing recipes for ice cream, published several times by the Nichols company in the 1930s.

The company made a cornflower-based powder 'under ideal conditions, untouched by hand', for the ice cream trade. The basic combination of the powder, boiled milk and sugar could be enriched with the addition of eggs, Nestlé's condensed milk or cream. The mixture was slowly frozen and turned with the aid of a special ice cream bucket which gave it a light and creamy texture.

Showcard, 1930s.

Carlo Tiani's ice cream cart, Ardwick, Manchester, 1928.

Until the Second World War ice cream was mainly made by Italian families, particularly around Manchester, in the Welsh valleys and Glasgow. Much of it was produced in the whitewashed cellars of their homes. They would then set off with colourful home-painted carts and wagons to collect some ice before touring the streets. They rang a bell to warn people of their arrival. The ice cream was at first sold in a glass cup, which was washed between each customer. Later, in the 1920s, the wafer and the cornet were introduced. Basins from home could also be filled with ice cream, which was better value.

Letterhead of P. Verrecchia, Glasgow, 1934.

The ice cream soda fountain had been introduced by Mr Selfridge from America when his new store opened in Oxford Street, London, in 1909. By the 1920s the ice cream parlour had become established as an institution. The Nichols company sold glass and white china ice cream shells, polished brass wafer holders and ice cream spoons, including the new 'one serve' wooden ones. Special syrups which were especially thick and sweet for the purpose were sold in a variety of flavours, including VIMTO, cream soda and lime. A cold float of ice cream made with sparkling VIMTO was popular during the summer months.

'If the weather was cold we could always go and fortify ourselves in Turner's temperance bar or Gotelli's ice cream shop with a good, hot, highly potent drink of VIMTO at two-pence a shot.'
Frank Findley on Harpurhey in the 1930s, *Days that Used to Be,* **1976 (unpublished).**

Cinema advert for Tognarelli's, Kendal, Cumbria, late 1920s.

T. C. Manfredi's Ice Cream Stores displaying VIMTO showcards, 1920s.

Going to the Pictures

The luxurious Plaza Cinema, Stockport, when it first opened in 1932.

By the 1920s a trip to the cinema was the most popular leisure pursuit. The silent black and white film created a magical world of make-believe, very different to what lay outside the cinema doors. This was despite the small flickering screen with ill-timed subtitles, accompanied by a single pianist. The arrival of the 'talkies' from America in 1928 saw the end of the silent film. The pictures had become the great escape for the majority of people. In the 1930s picture houses increased in quality and quantity. For 6d. (the price of a pint of beer) you could buy three hours of wall-to-wall carpeting, plush seating, warmth and privacy—all of which were still lacking in most homes.

VIMTO was advertised on a regular basis at the Plaza, which is now a bingo hall.

Cinema advert incorporating a showcard with an endorsement by the vivacious redheaded star of stage and screen, Elsie Randolph, mid-1930s.

In 1934, the Nichols company appointed the Manchester based Osborne-Peacock advertising agency. They arranged for famous stars to declare their support of the brand, no doubt for a fee.

Still from *Staleybridge Wakes Week*, 1927, showing children queuing for the matinée at the New Princess Cinema, Staleybridge.
This film was a publicity stunt by the cinema to attract the holiday makers away from the eight rival picture houses. The audience delighted in seeing themselves on the screen.

The Carlton Cinema Café, Salford, 1937.
The cinema café also often served VIMTO and made a good meeting place. The new Carlton Cinema described its café in the opening programme of 1937 as 'Light, airy and cosy, but not homely. Contrarily, it is a place where the homely and the exacting, the joyous and the jaded, may find change —something different—where they may find tempting food daintily served, renew an acquaintance, take a comfortable view of the world and his wife. And do it on prices light on the purse.'

Cinema advert, late 1920s.
VIMTO was advertised on the screen and sold in bottles in the auditorium. The film director Terence Davies wrote recently in *The Independent* on the difficulties of turning 'tiny shards of memory' into film. He recalled 'The boys, the laughter, VIMTO in a bottle' at the Savoy picture house in London in the 1950s.

The Sporting Life

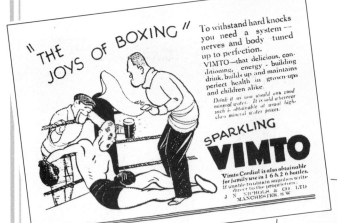

Newspaper advert, 1932.
Boxing was a popular sport of the working classes, and many a 'hungry boxer' escaped from the poverty of the slums through being a successful fighter.

Newspaper advert, 1929.
Running was a well-established form of exercise by the 1930s.

Newspaper advert, 1929.
Football had a working class image with the best players coming from the industrialised cities. The sin of gambling was added to the 'sin' of professionalism in the 1930s with the arrival of the Football Pools. The first World Cup was held in 1930, with 13 nations participating.

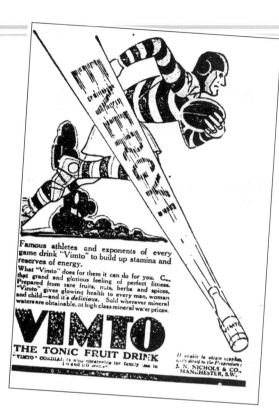

Newspaper advert, 1929.
The energising and stamina-building effects of VIMTO were often described.

The Nichols company 'Hi-Speed' range, 1985–9.
The popular modern sports of surfing, skiing and American football are depicted. This will be a visual source for the social historian in years to come.

Newspaper advert, 1956.
The association with glamorous and expensive sports such as that of driving racing cars is unusual in the range of advertising for VIMTO.

Hiking and Cycling

Cinema advert, late 1920s.
Hiking was all the rage in the 1930s. The word 'hiking',
meaning 'a fairly long walk', had been brought over
from America via the 'talkies'.

Trade advert, 1929 (detail).

'When cycling was a common pastime . . . we would have dozens calling in on their way
out, and, tired and thirsty, they would call in on their way home. At least two to one were in
favour of VIMTO.'
**Robert M. Scholey remembering the days in his father's herbalist shop on the
outskirts of Sheffield in the 1950s and '60s (1992).**

Advert in *The New Vimto Book
for Scholars*, 1939.

'OH! h'h' for a VIMTO'. Proof
(damaged) for a humorous
showcard, mid-1930s.

KEEP FIT AND WELL
Drink VIMTO

VIMTO should have its place in every
cyclist's kit. No more refreshing drink
was ever made. See how the miles fly
after a drink of this delicious stimula-
ting beverage !

If you haven't a bottle of VIMTO with
you when you go hiking, you will walk
all the faster to get to the nearest
source of supply. If you have VIMTO
with you, you will enjoy your hike
knowing that you can refresh yourself
anytime. VIMTO is so energising and
is so good for you !

Novelty postcard in which the sky was treated with a chemical which changed colour according to the humidity of the air, mid-1930s.

WHEN THE SKY ON THIS CARD IS BLUE, THE WEATHER WILL BE FINE. WHEN PINK, RAIN MAY BE EXPECTED. LILAC COLOUR INDICATES A CHANGE. THE WEATHER MAY BE CHANGEABLE, BUT THE QUALITY OF "VIMTO" NEVER VARIES — IT'S ALWAYS "FINE".

Showcard, 1947, harking back to pre-war imagery. It shows two bottles of the crimson brew perched precariously in the damsel's rucksack.

The first sip of VIMTO for some time put my mind into reverse motion. It is a sunny day and we are all going for a walk in Hindley's Borsdane Wood. Excited kids skipping down by the cemetery and then under the tunnels, after which a row of old houses come into sight. The sun has become hotter and we kids are thirsty. 'Yes we are, Mam.' Outside one of the cottages, a little sign advertising glasses of VIMTO for a penny.

Sitting there amongst the weeds— and as the year wore on in the shade of the purple willow herb—seem very ordinary. But viewed in the VIMTO light of forty years later, it seems magic.'
Geoffrey Shryhane writing in *The Wigan Observer* (1994).

Game, Set and Match

Women are indulging in strenuous sport more and more. So long as they take Vimto regularly, they can, because Vimto builds up stamina and gives reserves of energy.

BCM/VIMTO.

Vimto is a delicious and healthful drink. See that you get it, and bring the radiant glow of health to your cheeks! Sold wherever mineral waters are obtainable at usual high-class mineral water prices.

VIMTO
GIVES VIM TO YOU

Newspaper advert, 1928.
Tennis was another popular outdoor sport. It has been popularised by the Wimbledon Championships and the glamour of the tennis stars. It was especially enjoyed by women, who could now wear the more practical 'short frocks' or shorts. Anyone who could afford suitable clothing could play.

Showcard for Nichols 'Golden Vim' Grapefruit Crush depicting a tennis party in a well to do household, early 1930s.
The social side of playing sport was facilitated by soft drinks. The 1930s saw the rise in popularity of citrus fruit drinks. A lemon fruit 'squash' containing pulp and juice had been introduced from Australia just before the First World War. But it was to satisfy the public craze for eating citrus fruits for health that the 'Golden Vim' Crush range was created in 1930. The advertising claimed: 'The public will appreciate this easy way of taking grapefruit.'

SPARKLING
"Golden Vim" REGD
GRAPE FRUIT CRUSH

**INVIGORATING
REFRESHING
DELICIOUS**

Golf

Cinema advert, late 1920s.
Golf was mainly the sport of the middle classes and was also increasingly popular with women. Many new courses were opened in the expanding suburbs. The short baggy trouser fashion for men, 'plus-fours', was soon worn off the green more than on.

Showcard, mid-1920s.
A woman golfer is depicted in her fashionable cloche hat and short cropped hair.

Owzat?

Bottle display stand, early 1930s.
Cricket was a sport with universal appeal, and with good summers and great wickets, it had a golden age in the 1920s and '30s. The distinction between the gentlemen amateurs and the professional players was still maintained. Like football and rugby, local clubs thrived.

Novelty postcard, 1926.
As the wheel is rotated, the impression is given of the lad writing and rubbing off the slogans on the cricket scoreboard.

Showcard depicting a cricketer, mid-1920s.

Showcard by Stan Terry, early 1950s.

Cooling and Refreshing as a Dip in the Sea

Showcard, mid-1930s. The backless swimming costume, designed to maximise exposure to the sun, the style of shoe, and the crimped hairstyle are typical of the period.

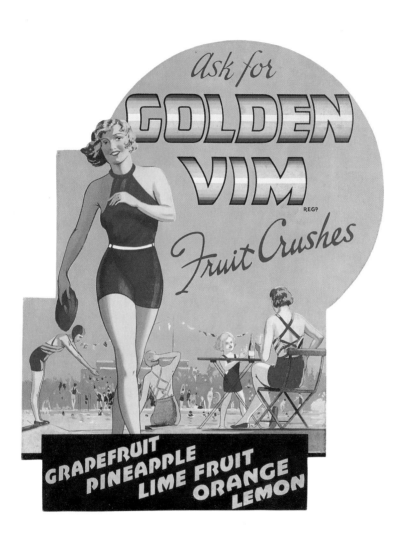

Showcard for the Nichols Golden Vim range, mid-1930s.
The 1920s and '30s saw the building of stylish outdoor swimming
complexes known as Lidos. The pools were surrounded with
fountains and flower beds, and provided plenty of space for
sunbathing around a variety of pools. They were cheap and open
long hours. Cafés were often attached to them.

Showcard commissioned by the Burma Ice and Aerated Water Company of Rangoon in 1927.
The format—of an engaging person holding up a bottle and a glass of VIMTO—is taken from the showcards issued by the Nichols company. However, it is a Burmese woman in local dress, accompanied by text in the local language and script, who presented the product.

Outdoor poster advertising VIMTO to the new Russian market, 1993.

Advert for VIMTO – 'The rarest of soft drinks' – in the *Times of India*, June 1954.

5

Famous Throughout The World

THE spices and herbs used to give VIMTO its distinctive flavour were imported from many parts of the world. In turn, the Nichols Company developed an important export market as the drink became popular abroad. By 1919 the first of many overseas trade mark registrations was made in British Guiana (now Guyana) and the company was soon describing itself in catalogues as a 'Wholesale Export Druggist'. A traveller who had taken a voyage around the world in 1930, looking for some VIMTO to sustain him, would have found it in at least thirty foreign lands. Countries as diverse as Peru, China, Albania and Liberia, along with the strongholds of the British Empire, found it 'most refreshing'. A fruity, thirst-quenching drink with an elusive flavour appealed to all cultures especially in countries with hot climates. It was also well respected as an English product, and local advertising emphasised its origins.

Local agents, who received a 5 per cent commission, would appoint mineral water manufacturers to bottle the drink, thus creating employment in the country concerned. Agents who were keen to show their success would send back promotional material and photographs of publicity events or trucks painted in the VIMTO livery. The photographs have been kept in a scrapbook and provide most of the illustrations for this chapter. Agents would also advise on the best packaging and labelling, as well as the style and language of advertising to suit the local culture, religion and politics of the country to whom it was appealing. It was not until 1955, when John Noel Nichols junior was taking over the export trade and air travel had become easier, that trips abroad were taken to experience the market first-hand.

British India

Early in the 1920s a friend of Noel Nichols, Mr Richard Goodsir, who was the Indian representative for Kiwi boot polish, said that he would like to take a few samples of VIMTO concentrate to India with him to see if he could interest the local bottling firms in the drink. He probably also took some of the labels and showcards to show that, once the drink was bottled, it could be easily promoted. Troops from the North West Regiments, who would already have been familiar with VIMTO, provided an immediate market. For a member of the 'British Other Ranks' on a five-year tour of India, isolated in a self-contained cantonment, VIMTO was certainly a taste of home.

In February 1924 the name was registered in India as a trade mark and soon the drink was appealing to the Indian palate. Its use rapidly spread, with the help of Mr Goodsir, to Burma (now Myanmar), Goa and Ceylon

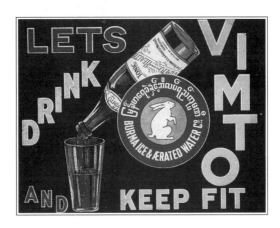

Showcard issued by the Burma Ice and Aerated Water Company, 1927.

(now Sri Lanka). Newspaper and cinema advertisements in English and the local languages and scripts emphasised the thirst-quenching quality of VIMTO which although non-alcoholic would give you 'vim' and 'pep'.

The name was registered as a trade mark in Burma in 1925, while the country was still part of British India. In 1927 Mr Goodsir was given power of attorney in order to protect the 'VIMTO' trade mark. In 1931 a legal battle ensued with the makers of a red drink called 'Venato'. The legal documents declared that VIMTO had extensive sales and had become famous throughout Burma, through the sale of both the carbonated drink and the cordial. The case rested upon the pronunciation of the names of the drinks. In the singing single-syllable-word language of Burmese, 'VIMTO' is pronounced 'Win-toe' and the rival name 'Venato' was pronounced 'Wee-ner-toe', with the second syllable glided over, so there was little difference between the two. The court decided in favour of the Nichols Company.

Twenty-gallon oak barrels of unsweetened double-strength concentrate were taken by the company's trucks to the docks at Liverpool while, like champagne, wooden cases of a dozen bottles of cordial were packed in straw sleeves. They were loaded on the ships and carried on well-established trade routes to India in vessels which, having brought raw cotton to the Lancashire cotton mills, would take back colourful printed cloth.

VIMTO was particularly popular in the Muslim area of the Indian sub-continent which in 1947 became Pakistan. Its appeal partly lay in the non-alcoholic nature of the beverage. Brian Blakeway served in the North West of Pakistan commanding the Royal Pakistan Engineer Regiment in the early 1950s. Every month the officers would hold a formal dinner night, at the end of which the President of Pakistan and H.M. the Queen were toasted. All of the other officers were true followers of Islam. He wrote in 1991—'We passed the VIMTO, properly decanted. And that "dark elixir" passed muster very well'.

Whereas many products left with the British on Indian independence in 1947, VIMTO remained. It ceased to be sold there in the late 1950s but current negotiations should see its re-introduction. The word 'VIMTO' has also become generic for any red soft drink in India and Pakistan. VIMTO is bottled legally in Karachi in Pakistan, but there are two imitations on the market which also call themselves 'VIMTO'. There are two court cases running, where the imitators claim that as 'VIMTO' is part of the local language, it has no significance as a registered trade mark. The Nichols company is defending its case strongly.

Advertisement in the *Friend of Burma*, May 1928.

The Middle East

Many Indian clerks, fluent in both Arabic and English, found employment in businesses in the Middle East in the 1920s. One particular family firm, Abdulla Aujan & Brothers, who had a successful grocery supply business in Bahrain, were introduced to VIMTO by one of their Indian employees. By 1928, large quantities of the cordial were being exported to them for distribution.

The popularity of the drink soon spread through their network of trading branches into the Arab States controlled by local sheikhs, such as Kuwait, Oman, Qatar, Dubai and Abu Dhabi. In 1933 the discovery of oil along the Persian Gulf ensured prosperity for the region. The luxuries of industrialised societies were in

'Open' and 'Closed' signs appearing in Aujan Soft Drink Industries Sales Development Manual, 1989.

greater demand as living standards rose. The inhabitants of the surrounding countries, Persia (now Iran), Iraq, Syria and the British colony and protectorate of Aden (now part of the Yemen Republic), also found the drink to their taste.

After the Second World War a shipping service to the Middle East was provided from Salford Docks. Brought into the port at Bahrain, wooden crates of cordial which had been packed into the bulkheads of ships were transported by water around the Gulf in Arab 'dhows'. By the 1960s pallet loads of VIMTO in cardboard boxes were being transported to the newly developed ports of Kuwait and the Trucial States.

The cordial which was exported was of double strength to cut down on transport costs. The sweetness also suited the Middle Eastern palate. It is sold to the public for drinking at home as well as being prepared for sale by drink sellers in the bustling bazaars. VIMTO is particularly popular during Ramadan for its restorative effect after fasting. In 1975 Solent Canners negotiated a licence to produce canned carbonated VIMTO for sale to Saudi Arabia and Kuwait, and later the United Arab Emirates. They were given the Queen's Award for Export Achievement in 1978 and 1979 on the strength of the Middle Eastern sales. The canning company was acquired by Nichols in 1980.

In the 1970s duties were levied on goods imported into Saudi Arabia, so in 1979 the Aujan family was licensed to bottle cordial in the country itself. In 1980, 120 million filled cans of VIMTO were exported to the Middle East. This figure further justified the decision to build an on-the-spot canning line in Saudi Arabia, as this would substantially reduce transportation costs and duty. The new Aujan Soft Drinks Industries company was formed as part of the Aujan group, which is still run by the same family. The price of VIMTO was lowered as a result and the market share, against its main competitor, Pepsi-Cola, was increased.

Until the 1980s the production of point-of-sale material and cinema advertisements was handled in Britain by Royds advertising agency, dependent on Arabic translators. Nowadays the marketing and promotion of the drink is left to the Aujan family. As in this country, the cordial has a family market, while the canned carbonates are for the younger drinker. In a recent television commercial for VIMTO cordial, the eldest son dressed in a suit returns home for a family gathering where the dress is traditional. The equivalent advertisement for the canned drink shows the younger brother returning to join his friends and girlfriend for a party on the beach. No women are allowed in television advertisements during Ramadan so edited versions showing only men are screened during this prime sales period.

In 1990, a new can design was introduced. The new upper and lower case diagonal scripting of the VIMTO name used in Britain was rejected in market research as people either did not like it or did not recognise the name. The block capital lettering, which had acted as a logo, was retained but taken diagonally up the side of the red can. Some of the fruit ingredients were depicted, before their introduction in the current UK packaging.

During the uncertain period of the Gulf War, the only major market affected was that in Kuwait. A greetings card was sent from an American soldier, Sgt Terry D. Johnson, who had sampled VIMTO in Saudi Arabia during Operation Desert Storm. He wanted to know where he could obtain supplies back in America.

North America and Canada

Trade magazines in America carried advertisements seeking bottling agents as early as 1925 but, despite VIMTO being described as 'The Business Maker . . . A Drink with sales exceeding 17 million bottles annually', there were no takers. An agent who surveyed the American soft drink market in 1929 reported that Coca-Cola was the most popular beverage and sent back some samples of other drinks. In 1931 Noel Nichols and his accountant and fellow director, John Stewart-Smith, decided to make a trip to America and Canada to muster business. They also wanted to purchase raw materials such as Californian grape seed oil. They did not have any success in America. The local mineral water manufacturers thought that there were already similar drinks on the market and that they could make something very much the same themselves. Toronto in Canada, however, was happy to try the drink. A poor reproduction

The Nichols Company international collection of fake VIMTO cordial bottles,
with an original of the early 1980s in the foreground.

of a catalogue from the 1930s shows a fleet of eight trucks all painted with the words 'Drink "VIMTO" costing 5 cents'. Today, after a gap of fifty years, VIMTO is again sold in the Eastern Provinces of Canada in cans.

In the 1970s VIMTO finally found a niche in the biggest soft drink market in the world, America. Initially, importers of British foods such as English marmalade and McVities digestive biscuits included VIMTO cordial in their range. In 1980 the 7-UP company was distributing cordial and sparkling VIMTO and promoting the drink on the radio. For a time VIMTO was also imported as a temperance beverage for the Mormons in Salt Lake City. More recently the cordial version of the drink was promoted by Segrew Importers, New Jersey. VIMTO was marketed as 'The Case of the Elusive Flavour' which Sherlock Holmes was trying to solve.

Europe

The year 1991 saw the introduction of sparkling VIMTO in cans and bottles to France, Spain and Portugal. It was described on the French standard and 'diet' bottle as 'Nouveau VIMTO Soda aux Fruits Rouge' and 'Une boisson unique au gout inoubliable'. The English expression 'light' distinguishes the 'diet' version. The Spanish can labelling called it a 'Refrescante VIMTO refresco aromatizado'. The packaging and label design are similar to the UK versions. So far in Europe the Britishness of the drink has not been emphasised to the extent it has been in other continents.

All over the world

Today VIMTO is still sold in over thirty countries and the trade mark is registered in over seventy places in the world. This is to cover the bordering countries as well as the main markets, as the label and product have been fraudulently imitated many times. Over 50 per cent of the finished product is drunk abroad, 80 per cent of this in the Middle East. The export trade is an ever-changing one. The company has been frustrated on occasion because, having created a demand for VIMTO, foreign governments apply import restrictions or heavy duties. Local agents sometimes have difficulty in obtaining import licences.

Old markets such as Cyprus and Trinidad have been revived, whereas exports have only just started to countries such as the Morocco and Angola. Negotiations are under way in Vietnam, the Czech Republic and Slovakia. In Russia, shops and kiosks are now gradually stocking cans of sparkling VIMTO. The 'Ain't That a Shame' commercial is being adapted for the local market to support the launch. The soft drink has become a symbol of a certain quality of life. Australia and New Zealand have as yet to be introduced formally to VIMTO. It is, however, drunk there on a small scale by many 'pommies' who have settled and taken back a bottle of cordial after a visit to the UK.

VIMTO is described and pronounced in many different ways and is packaged and advertised with great diversity. However, the fascinating taste has captured many palates and continues to be 'famous throughout the world'.

India – the First Export Market

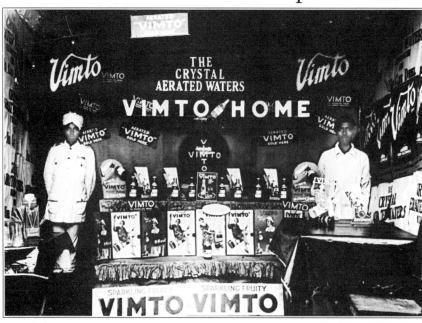

Exhibition stand of The Crystal Aerated Waters Company in Vizianagram, India, late 1930s. Showcards and posters supplied by the Nichols company decorate the stand.

Hajoori & Sons adorned their delivery van on a VIMTO theme for the Hindu Ashtami Fair, Surat, in 1933.

Showcard which appears in photographs of local events in the 1930s sent in by agents abroad, including British India and Tanganyika (now Tanzania).
The girl is dressed in Harliquinade costume and smokes a cigarette in the days when the addiction could still accompany the slogan 'Keeps You Fit'.

The winners of the Grand Advertising Ball, Lahore (now in Pakistan), held for Earthquake Relief Fund, 1930.
The Teplitz Aerated Water Company awarded prizes to the people whose costumes best represented well-advertised products, including VIMTO. VIMTO had been introduced into India in the early 1920s and by 1927 a newspaper advert declared it was 'For Everybody in India'.

Advert shown in cinemas in Madras, early 1930s.

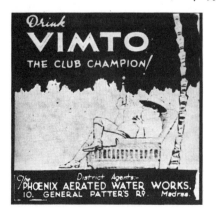

The Middle East

Shelf talker with the text 'The Joy of Gathering—VIMTO', used in Saudi Arabia during Ramadan in 1986.
VIMTO was introduced to the Middle East in 1927 by Indian clerks. A grocery supply business run by the Aujan family in Bahrain soon distributed VIMTO cordail throughout the region, where it is still very popular today. In the whole of the ninth month of the Muslim year no food or drink is allowed during hours of daylight. A fresh date is the traditional way in which they break their Ramadan fast and many also have a strong glass of VIMTO cordial to quickly restore lost energy and liquid. Sales during Ramadan account for 60 per cent of the annual figure. In 1976 carbonated VIMTO in special red Arabic cans became available. The familiar cordial bottle was incorporated into the design.

Cartoon illustrating the Middle East export market which accompanied a financial article on J. N. Nichols (VIMTO) plc, 1984.

Street advert for a consumer competition which featured three jeeps as prizes, Saudi Arabia, 1993.

Egypt

Entrant to a fancy dress competition, Cairo, 1930s.

An outlet for VIMTO in Alexandria, Egypt, 1930s.

Delivery carts in Alexandria, Egypt, 1947.
VIMTO was bottled in Alexandria by Les Fils de Paschal Elia from the 1930s through to the Suez crises of the 1950s. Since 1993, both the cordial and sparkling VIMTO have been bottled there again.

Africa and Cyprus

The staff of Patwas Minerals in fancy dress, Tanganyika, early 1950s.

Once a year the staff wore fancy dress and decorated their delivery vans with a VIMTO theme for a local carnival. VIMTO was sold in many parts of Africa from 1928 onwards. Apart from Liberia and Egypt, the countries were then the colonies of Britain, France and Belgium. It is still very popular in East and West Africa today.

The captain of the VIMTO Lake Football Trophy, Tanganyika, in 1956.

Local agents arrange sponsorship of events and sporting activities as a way of promoting the drink. As in Britain, sports are sponsored, and 'The VIMTO Trophy' was the prize for an annual football match held during the 1950s. More recently, in 1993, a three-day car rally was sponsored by Zhara Bottlers as part of their promotion of the VIMTO brand.

Young customers enjoy a VIMTO in a café in Nicosia, Cyprus, late 1940s.

A showcard declares that VIMTO is 'Back Again', after the break in the export trade during the Second World War.

The Far East

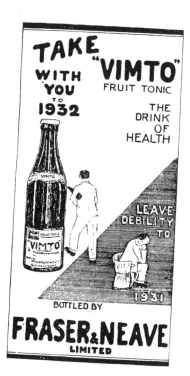

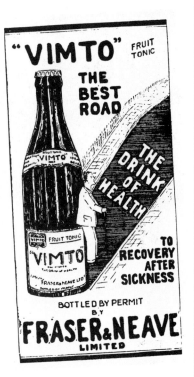

Newspaper adverts published by Fraser and Neave Ltd, Singapore, 1932.
In Singapore, Malaya (now Malaysia), Java and Dutch East India (now Indonesia), the bottling agent Fraser and Neave sold VIMTO from 1931 through to the late 1940s, with a gap during the Second World War. They used showcards sent out from the UK, but also did their own advertising. A series of poorly drawn but poignant newspaper adverts promoted the tonic properties of VIMTO for 'recovery after sickness', 'an antidote to work weariness' and as an aid to leaving the debility of 1931.

Still for an advertising film shown throughout cinemas in Malaya and Dutch East India in October 1940.
It featured a couple enjoying a VIMTO standing together behind the bar. A selection of showcards, of which there are examples in The VIMTO Advertising Collection, are displayed. They had all been designed originally for the British market.

South America

Display for an exhibition stand of the Minerva Aerated Water Company, Peru, early 1930s, featuring VIMTO and 'Vita-Cola'. Sparkling VIMTO was bottled by local plants along the whole north and west coasts of Central and South America, including the Spanish-speaking republics of Columbia, Ecuador, Peru and Chile.

First-class diploma awarded at the Grand National Exhibition at Bogotá, Columbia, 1931. The 'agua de frutas VIMTO' was a great success and was awarded several diplomas and medals in the early 1930s despite strong competition from American beverages.

South American showcard, early 1930s.
The same showcard design was used in Britain.

Leaflets freely distributed at religious festivals, 1931.
A religious scene appeared on one side, with a poem in Spanish praising VIMTO on the reverse. The translation reads:
'Good Advice. In intense heat, never drink liquor. Your liver suffers if you drink spirits, and if you drink a lot of beer you become very lazy. The way to refresh yourself without getting drunk is to ask for delicious VIMTO, with its delightful flavour. You'll never find another drink which equals VIMTO, the ideal.'

The Caribbean

VIMTO **Kite Flying Competition, British Guiana (now Guyana), Easter 1940.**
British Guiana was the first country abroad in which VIMTO was registered as a trade mark, in 1919. Little is known about the early days of the market, but by 1928 barrels of double-strength VIMTO concentrate were being exported to other parts of the region, including El Salvador, Costa Rica, Dutch Guiana (now Surinam) and the British islands of the West Indies. In 1940 D'Aguia Bros Ltd in British Guiana held a grand kite competition. The 500 kites were provided free with the purchase of VIMTO, and the winner flying the highest kite would be decided by three judges, one of whom was the enigmatic 'Mr Art Williams (aeronautic expert) if in town'.

Publicity photograph for VIMTO cordial in the Caribbean, 1991.
A newspaper report in Trinidad in 1932, which one suspects may have been written by the VIMTO agent, said that the 'younger, fashionable set have taken to toasting one another with that new drink'—VIMTO. Today the drink is promoted in a similar way.

Advert from the official brochure of the Thirst Park company, Georgetown, Guyana, 1970 who were the then bottling agents for VIMTO.

..the favorite!
VIMTO

North America

Leaflet advertising VIMTO in America, 1990 (detail).

Although VIMTO was registered as a trademark in America as early as 1921, and regular attempts were made to attract bottling agents, VIMTO cordial and carbonate were not available in the States until the 1970s. More recently the cordial version of the drink was promoted by Segrew Importers, New Jersey, who described it as 'The great non-alcoholic drink from England' with much prestige. Its versatility to be served as a 'hot toddy' or 'with selzer' was described. The fact that it is caffeine free, has vitamin C and is not as high in calories as many American soft drinks are all in its favour. A stylish black and gold label was printed to include a moated castle. The VIMTO name appeared in medieval script and the brand even had acquired its own coat of arms!

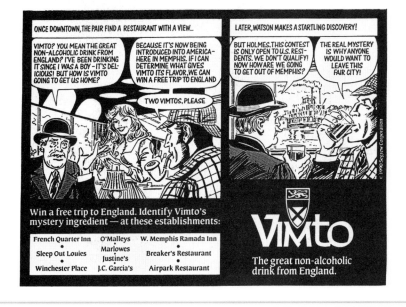

Publicity leaflet entitled 'Can Sherlock Holmes solve Memphis' Greatest Mystery?', issued by Segrew Corporation in Memphis, Tennessee, in 1990 (detail).

LEFT. Kerry Morrison carving a grape from an oak log with a chain-saw at the Haydock distribution warehouse, March 1992. The wood came from sustainable forests.

A Monument to Vimto, 1992, on the campus lawn at UMIST.

6

A Monument to VIMTO

IT WAS in the course of research for the travelling exhibition, *Vimto—The Story of a Soft Drink*, that I discovered that Manchester, rather than Salford, was the true birthplace of VIMTO. Up to that point, Chapel Street in Salford had always been referred to as the company's first address. However, in discussion with the former chief chemist, Joe Pearson, it was revealed that the first premises were in Granby Row, Manchester, albeit only for two years. Joe had been a student at the nearby Manchester Municipal College of Technology (now UMIST) and remembered the company's first employee, Tom Broadhurst, talking about the early days. Tom had been fined for playing football in Granby Row. The dates were confirmed by the first catalogue of goods for sale which turned up in the company archives. It gave the address as 49 Granby Row and was dated 1908 in the handwriting of Noel Nichols. *Slater's Manchester, Salford and Suburban Directory* of January 1909, recording householders and businesses street by street of the previous year, further confirmed the fact. Ordnance Survey maps of 1911 and 1913 located the exact spot.

I went along to see if the building was still there to photograph it. I also had at the back of my mind the thought of perhaps placing a blue plaque on the wall to mark the invention of VIMTO. The more substantial buildings of Granby Row such as Orient House were still standing but the warehouses and industrial buildings of the block in which 49 Granby Row had stood had been demolished in the 1960s. The site had become the leafy campus lawn of the University of Manchester Institute of Science and Technology. Two sculptures, *Technology Arch* by Axel Wolkenhauer (1988) and *Archimedes* by Thomas Dagnell (1990) had already been commissioned by UMIST as a result of a sculpture competition. 'A Monument to VIMTO' suggested itself as an idea.

After the notion was accepted by the management of the company, a telephone call to UMIST was made to establish who owned the land and to put the idea to them. Iain McMullan, the Director of Development and Tony Pass, UMIST's architect, welcomed the suggestion.

After the initial meeting and agreement to go ahead with the project, it was decided to hold a competition as the subject was so novel and open to wide interpretation. It was restricted to sculptors and craftspeople working in the North West of England, partly to keep the number of entrants manageable and partly to reflect the origins of the drink. Details of the competition were placed in *Artists' Newsletter*, to which there was an excellent and interesting response. There were several applications from artists outside the region to remove the geographical restriction, but these were reluctantly turned away.

Model by Kerry Morrison, painted plaster and mixed media, 1991–2. Kerry Morrison designed her stained oak sculpture to reflect the essence of VIMTO with enormous carved fruits and spices arranged around a bottle of sparkling VIMTO set upon a platter.

In November 1991 a panel of seven had the task of shortlisting six artists to put forward ideas. Professor Christopher Rose-Innes, himself an artist and Virginia Tandy from North West Arts Board joined Iain McMullan, Tony Pass, John Nichols, Simon Nichols and myself at UMIST to choose from the entrants. The six sculptors chosen were Jon Biddulph, Jon Cattan, Lorna Green, Andrew Holmes, Kerry Morrison and Richard Thornton. Between them they had a great variety of experience, styles and media but all had shown imagination and ingenuity in their work. The six were commissioned to make a model and at least one sketch outlining their idea of a suitable monument to VIMTO. They were required to visit the travelling exhibition on VIMTO for background information and possible inspiration. The budget was £15,000, to include all materials, expenses and the artist's fee.

On 7 January 1992 we waited in anticipation as the artists brought their work into the boardroom at the Wythenshawe office. Their ideas were exhibited soon after at the City Art Gallery in Manchester. It proved a very popular exhibition with the public. They were asked for their choice and comments on the proposals. Opinions varied enormously and the comments were taken into account by members of the panel when they met within the exhibition space on 10 February 1992 to determine the final choice of sculptor.

The subject, materials and suitability for the site of each of the ideas were thoroughly discussed. Eventually the final choice was Kerry Morrison's large-scale bottle and fruit carved in oak. Kerry, who was born in 1965, had recently completed an M.A. in Site Specific Sculpture at the Wimbledon School of Art. She had already been commissioned for several site specific outdoor public sculptures in wood. In 1990 she was awarded the Prince's Trust 'Go and See' grant to visit European sculptors.

Kerry set to work with her chain saw on oak trunks taken from trees grown in the carefully managed commercial forests of Henry Venables and National Trust properties. The finer carving on the raspberries, blackcurrants and stalks was done with a chisel and hammer. Most of the work was carried out at the VIMTO central distribution warehouse at Haydock, where there was an outdoor space and a garage for storing the finished work. Ample supplies of VIMTO quenched Kerry's thirst as she performed her hot and heavy task of forming the enormous fruits, vanilla pods and bottle.

In just four months Kerry had finished the work ready for the unveiling on 9 July by Barbara Knox (alias Rita Sullivan, formerly Fairclough) from *Coronation Street*. The most famous corner shop owner in Britain declared the sculpture open with

Kerry Morrison supervising the installation of the bottle, July 1992. The staining, preservative and sun-screen treatments were carried out beforehand, with the label being painted on site.

a reproduction of one of the 'Open … Closed' signs from the VIMTO advertising collection.

The rich red and dark brown tones of the stained and treated oak blend well with the backdrop of the red brick and terracotta UMIST main building. The natural material is suitable to the nature of the green site of the campus lawn between the building and the railway viaduct. Oak is warm and inviting, particularly in the harsh environment of the city. The subject is immediate and traditional, and almost has the overall impression of a sepia photograph. Kerry

had been inspired by images from the advertising collection such as a bottle on a tray or bowls of cascading fruit. One visitor to the City Art Gallery exhibition, Robert Scholey, had written the comment 'When I saw the model, I at once felt that I was back my father's herbalist shop. It brought back memories of the wonderful herby smells and that distinctive aroma VIMTO has.' Yet the scale of the sculpture and its subject on an inner-city site makes it arresting and modern. It truly is a monumental work of art fulfilling its purpose and title.

Monumental Ideas

Illustration and photomontage by Lorna Greene depicting her proposed bronze sculpture on the site of 49 Granby Row, near the UMIST main building, 1991–2.

Lorna Greene based her design on the form of the VIMTO cordial bottle. She divided up the shape vertically and the segments of the bottle gradually turned into the petals of the flowers of the fruits which make up VIMTO. The letters V I M T O soon became the stamens of the flowers. Her sculpture would have been in bronze, surrounded by rocks and pebbles in keeping with the natural site.

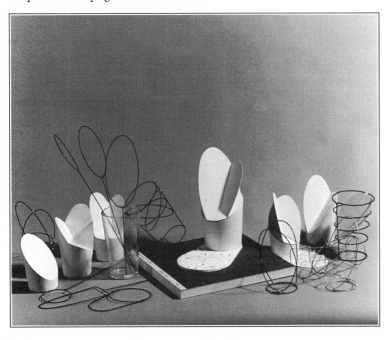

Working models and wire 'drawings' by Jon Biddulph, 1991–2 (card, plaster and wire).

The idea behind this sculpture was derived from memories of drinking VIMTO as a child, together with the notion of the first glass of VIMTO being held up to the light, tilted and drunk. The upright form is made of three intersecting ellipses describing the various liquid levels formed in a tilted glass. The horizontal shadow of the glass was made up of casts of toys and games. The sculpture would have been made of white concrete and quartz and floodlit at night with a ruby light.

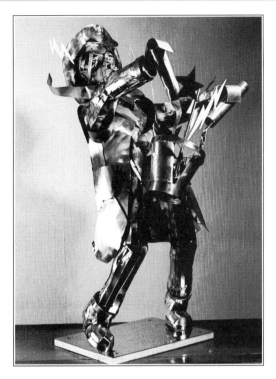

Model of John Noel Nichols mixing his first batch of VIMTO by Richard Thornton, 1991–2 (polished and painted stainless steel).

Richard Thornton depicted the entrepreneur at the exciting moment when he had discovered the magic drink. Made from polished and brightly painted stainless steel, the character would have had vitality and movement and be reminiscent of the early VIMTO showcards.

Model of 'Atlas' by Jon Cattan, 1991–2 (carved polystyrene foam).

Jon Cattan planned a bronze sculpture of Atlas who, in need of a rest, had sat upon his burden of the world to have a welcome drink of VIMTO. Jon liked the idea of using a classical theme to complement the local Victorian architecture, and was influenced by the humorous adverts for VIMTO used in the past.

Model of the ruins of 49 Granby Row by Andrew Holmes, 1991–2 (wood and mixed media).

Andrew Holmes wished to re-create the original building where VIMTO was first mixed in the form of a ruined brick and stone folly.

Recipe ideas for Vimto cordial

The obvious uses of VIMTO cordial are to dilute it to make a long cool drink, a hot winter warmer or a refreshing sparkling drink with the addition of soda or mineral water. The neat cordial, however, has many other uses in the kitchen in both sweet and savoury dishes. The following ideas have been compiled with the help of the International Catering Consultant, Tom Bridge M.C.F.A. (C.G.), Dr Lesley Petrie and Segrew Importers, the VIMTO agents in America. VIMTO drinkers have also made their contribution.

Savoury notions

Add VIMTO to a glaze and sauce for cooked ham.

Liven up braised cabbage by adding VIMTO when the stock is reduced. Garnish with raisins and chopped shallots.

Roast duck can be accompanied by a VIMTO and blackcurrant or cherry sauce.

An unusual hollandaise sauce seasoned with VIMTO tops off broccoli.

Hot vegetable soup or cold gazpacho soup can be enriched with a dash of VIMTO. Gazpacho soup can be garnished with VIMTO ice cubes.

Cream of stilton and mock port soup uses VIMTO as an excellent port substitute.

VIMTO can be added to a marinade for breast of duck.

Enhance a red pepper mousse with VIMTO.

VIMTO works well with crab meat cooked in Creole style.

Sweet delights

Blend VIMTO into your favourite cheesecake recipe.

Cherries or strawberries soaked in VIMTO make a luscious topping.

Use neat as a topping for ice cream, pancakes or waffles.

Just a dash in stewed fruit gives extra, exotic flavour.

Make an apricot and VIMTO puree as a basis for an unusual fool.

For delicious summer puddings, add VIMTO cordial to soft fruits.

Gelatine, sugar and VIMTO make a jelly that is really mouth-watering.

Sorbets and ice cream is sensational with VIMTO.

And VIMTO in yoghurt and milk puddings makes a change.

Soak trifle sponges with VIMTO instead of the more traditional jelly.

VIMTO and gelatine make a terrific quick glaze for fruit tarts and flans.

Steaming a fruit pudding? Add a dash of VIMTO.

Add VIMTO to waffle or crepe batter.

VIMTO colours and flavours home-made coconut ice and marshmallows.

Add VIMTO to icing for really special cakes.

VIMTO keeps Christmas cakes and puddings moist and full of flavour.

Use VIMTO where a recipe indicates cochineal—try chocolate and VIMTO marble cake for an unusual and delicious combination of flavours.

Colour and flavour desiccated coconut with VIMTO to sprinkle on top of coconut cake.

Make your own raisin bread with VIMTO.

Add slowly to thick whipped cream for a super topping.

VIMTO milkshake or yoghurt drink are brilliant!

Add VIMTO to lemonade or soda with a scoop of ice cream for a delicious summer cooler.

Cheers!

A slice of lemon and/or cinnamon stick enhances the taste of hot VIMTO.

A tablespoon of VIMTO in a cup of black tea makes an interesting change. Lemon optional.

VIMTO cordial mixes well with orange juice; lime juice and soda; ginger ale; Bacardi or vodka; rum, especially as a hot drink; champagne, to put it in the pink

Having a party? VIMTO makes a splendid base for fruit punch.

Sparkling VIMTO

The following are established regional favourites:

A 'Macki-Vim' is a VIMTO mixed with a Mackeson Stout in the Midlands.

A 'Scrumpy Tan' is with Cider in Somerset.

A 'Pink Velvet' is a mix of Guinness and sparkling VIMTO.